MICHAEL, M[...]
WHY DO YOU HATE ME?

by the Reverend Michael Esses

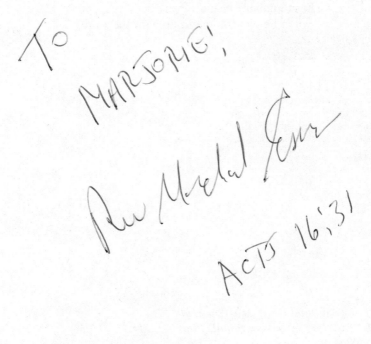

To MARJORIE,

Rev Michael Esses

Acts 16:31

LOGOS INTERNATIONAL

Plainfield, New Jersey

All Scriptures are quoted from the King James Version of the Holy Bible.

To our son, Donald Gard Esses
whose ministry began December 18, 1968
when he went home to be with the Lord

Michael, Michael, Why Do You Hate Me?
© *1973 by Logos International, Plainfield, N.J.   07060*
All Rights Reserved
Printed in the United States of America
ISBN: 0-88270-046-4 (hardcover)
        0-88270-074-2 (paper)

Introduction

How the Lord God loves the Jew! Ever since His promise to Abraham — indeed, since before the foundations of the world were laid — He has ordained and loved these chosen people.

He has poured out His affection, His provision, His power, His very heart upon this proud, child-like, impulsive, wayward, creative but stubborn people!

He loves all His children — but there's something special in His feeling for the Jew.

His love isn't cheap; it demands faith. His special favor comes at a very high price — *obedience.*

And that obedience so often makes no sense to the rational mind.

Abraham is called the "father of the faithful" because *"he believed in the Lord;* and He counted it to him for righteousness" (Gen. 15:6).

Look at the impossible things Abraham was expected to believe! That God wanted him to pack his considerable belongings and his family and leave his ancestral home toward a totally unknown destination! That he would have a son in his advanced old age — and that through him "all the nations of the earth would be blessed!" That after this

promise was given Abraham was to submit to the pain and
humiliation of *circumcision*—at the age of 99!

And finally, after the promised son arrived and grew into
young manhood, Abraham was required to *kill* that son as
a sacrifice to God!

Could *you* believe God through such "unreasonable"
promises and demands?

Abraham did.

And orthodox rabbi Michael Esses did—finally.

That's what thrills me about Mike's story. *His is a mod-
ern-day parable of the history of the people of Israel*—
lived in the life of one man.

Born in orthodoxy, taught the law of God as a child,
rebellious to the point of near suicide, he abandoned his
heritage, recklessly pursued pleasure and material success
—then met sudden crisis and eventual despair.

And then the miraculous intervention of God—and
Messianic deliverance!

I've grown to love my brother Mike, this impulsive,
headstrong, rambunctious, child-like, ever-maturing, God-
loving, courageous son of Israel.

I think you will, too. Go with him on his personal exodus
out of bondage from Syria, to Brooklyn, to California and
finally to Israel through the hectic wilderness of his life—
on his way to a moment of electrifying personal confrontation with the Lord, and his entrance into the Kingdom.

You may never be the same.

I myself have been changed by his story. It's very clear
that God has chosen Michael Esses, singled him out, given
him something special to do. And as always, He has demanded the high price of faith—and obedience.

Rabbi Mike may help you, as he has me, an adopted
Jew, to more closely identify with the "father of the
faithful":

"By faith Abraham, when he was called to go out into a

place which he should after receive for an inheritance, obeyed; and he went out, not knowing where he went.

By faith, he sojourned in the land of promise, as in a foreign country, dwelling in tents with Issac and Jacob, the heirs with him of the same promise;

For he looked for a city which hath foundations, whose builder and maker is God."

— Paul's letter to the Hebrews, 11:8–10.

Pat Boone

MICHAEL, MICHAEL,
WHY DO YOU HATE ME?

1

"LORD, hasten Your Messiah and next year in Jerusalem." This ancient Hebrew prayer, said each year by all Jews at Passover, is ringing over and over in my ears. Now the muffled, barely discernible call from American Airlines starts to play a duet with this prayer in my mind.

"American Airlines Flight 405 boarding at gate seventeen for New York will be delayed one hour." What a discordant note this is! At last I'm on my way to Jerusalem, and I couldn't be more anxious and excited. Even an hour's delay is too much.

I look around and start checking all the members of the tour I'm leading. I wonder what this trip will mean to most of them. I know for some it's an answer to many years of prayer and longing. To some, it's a pleasure trip, with most of the ladies looking forward to all the interesting shops. For others, it is an escape from unsolved problems that they are hoping will have mysteriously disappeared by the time they arrive back home. For me, it is a journey back to the very origin of my being.

My fellow tour members seem to be taking the delay in their stride. They've scattered in all directions. The momentum I have been under since I awoke this morning is subsiding, so I decide to find a comfortable chair and relax. I find one in the corner, out of all the hustle and bustle that's going on. Once I've sunk into the chair, I lean back and let my mind wonder about the many, many generations of Jews before me that have culminated with me sitting here, waiting to leave for Jerusalem.

The radically modern vista of Los Angeles International Airport seems to fade from my vision, and in my imagination I become a Hebrew child being led into captivity in the year 586 B.C. . . .

I stumble along at my mother's side, with my fist clenched in the folds of her dress. There is only one question in my mind. Why?

2

WHY IS this happening to us? Why are we so hated? Why do I have to leave my home and all that I love? There seems no way that my small mind can understand this persecution.

There is only one possibility. My father, Isaac Ben Judah—maybe he can give me an answer I can understand. My eyes dart here and there, searching the crowd for him. I see him helping a woman replace some bundles that have fallen from her cart. She is crying, and I can see the anguish on her face. My father speaks softly to her, and she reaches for his hand to kiss it. As Father turns toward my mother and me, my heart starts to pound in hopes that he can soothe me as he did the woman with the cart.

My father, Isaac, is one of the elders of the tribe of Judah. I have always looked at him with a mixture of awe and love. He is always the rock of strength I can turn to when there is trouble from my childish pranks or a need for compassion and understanding, that all children require in large doses. I know if anyone has the answer to our dilemma, it will be my father. As he approaches, he can see the total lack of understanding on my face. His hand is extended to me, and as he takes me into his arms, he tells me through my tears the story of a disobedient people and the results of their folly.

3

"Son, do you recall the great prophet Jeremiah whom the Lord spoke through many, many times? He warned our people that the Lord God was going to scatter our nation because of the many grievous sins they have been committing. You know of the prevalence of idols that our people have been worshiping. You have seen, amongst people you know, fathers who have sacrificed their children to false gods. Your mother and I have tried to shield you from these people, but you are a wise child and are aware of the many sins that are being committed.

"Many years ago, the prophet Amos warned that Israel would be scattered 'like as corn is sifted in a sieve.' At that time, the destruction of Israel by Assyria began. Now begins the destruction of Judah 135 years later.

"You have been taught by your rabbis (teachers) the lesson that as long as man walks with God in the paths of righteousness, all is well with him; but no sooner does he deviate therefrom than he becomes subject to the wrath of God. This is true for all men.

"We as a people have totally failed God. The sinfulness of idolatry in all its forms, the duty of wholehearted devotion to the laws of God, the maintenance of His worship in spirit and in truth—all these are fully recorded in His word. As with the individual, a people's obedience to God is rewarded by national security and prosperity, while disobedience is punished by national calamity.

"You have seen all around you the hypocrisy of the sanctuaries crowded with worshipers, with the altars piled high with sacrifices, while injustice, oppression, adultery, and even murder have gone unchecked. Religion has had no effect upon conduct, and our people have failed to understand that public as well as private life must be based on God's commandments.

"Our people have refused to listen to every prophet's warning that their sins would inevitably lead to national disaster and that trust in God and obedience to *His will* was the only course to follow.

"Jeremiah has come to the elders of our tribe and given us the Word of the Lord. God has told our people of Judah to surrender willingly into the hands of the Babylonians, and if we obey, the Lord has promised that he will rebuild the Temple Nebuchadnezzar was permitted to destroy, but if we persist in our arrogance and stay in Jerusalem, we will surely die.

"So you see, my son, as people who fear God—even though many of our own family have been disobedient to His laws—we must now be obedient and go willingly into captivity. For to be disobedient now is certain death. I know that many of our people in the coming years will say to themselves, 'Had we to do it over again, or given a second chance, we would be obedient to the Word of God.' "

Obedience, obedience, obedience—this word goes over and over in my mind like a broken record. The many times of disobedience and the few times of obedience in my life.

I slowly find myself coming back into focus, and am aware of people hurrying around, picking up their hand luggage. I feel a touch on my shoulder; it's my wife, telling me to wake up, it's time to board. There's no time to tell her I haven't been asleep, just many, many years in the past re-living a traumatic time with one of my ancestors. I know she would have a hard time understanding how each experience that a Jew has is somehow stamped on all future generations. These people are not remote to us, but are like our neighbors that we know today. We identify with them.

At last we're all on board, the excitement of takeoff is over, and everyone has settled down with their conversations, their books, and the myriad of things people find to do to pass the time while they cross this vast country.

When you compare the size of this country and that of the region where my people came from, the holy lands are lost, but the richness of their history and their people can't be denied. We in this wonderful country cannot imagine what it is like to roam from land to land or to settle in any land where we are hated.

3

MY ANCESTORS were faithful to the word of the Scriptures, and they stayed the full seventy years in captivity in Babylon. Some of our tribe of Judah went back to Jerusalem with the first group, with Zerubbabel, the prince of Judah. Some went back with Ezra, the prophet, and some went back with Nehemiah. My ancestors stayed in and around Babylon. Subsequently, they migrated to the northern part of Syria, to a city on the caravan routes called Aleppo. At one time, Aleppo was the capital of Syria.

My ancestors lived there from the year 516 B.C. to the year 1902 A.D., when my father came to the United States. Most of these men became strict Orthodox rabbis. Even though they were persecuted, they never gave up the God of Abraham, Isaac, and Jacob.

It is a Jewish phenomenon that every time you try to stamp out their faith with persecution and violence, you will find them clinging to it stronger than ever before. You can make them fourth-class citizens, you can herd them into ghettos, you can even destroy them and their families in gas chambers, but they will not abandon their God.

I know very little about my paternal grandfather, Abood, except that he was a rabbi. He was a man who had four wives, not that he had gone back to the sin of multiple wives, but because each successive wife died in childbirth. I know that death at childbirth was not an unusual happening in that day, but I think my grandfather decided he was a jinx after the fourth time, and decided to raise his children by himself. He had four sons, each by a different wife. There was David, who immigrated to the United States and died of diabetes when I was a child; Saleem, who also immigrated to the United States and died here at seventy-five years of age; Alfred, who died in Syria as a young man; and my father, Isaac.

My father, the youngest of the sons, was four years old when grandfather died, and his maternal grandmother took him to raise in the nurture and admonition of the Lord. This led him to become a rabbi in the footsteps of his ancestors. Such an undertaking would have been impossible for almost anybody, more so for an elderly woman, unless it was with the help of the Lord. My grandmother claimed that help.

At this particular time, Syria was under the domination of the Turkish Ottoman Empire, which not only persecuted their Jews, but their Christians as well. It seems that when man's inhumanity to man prevails, the first thing he does is try to wipe out, burn, and destroy the living Word of God, the Scriptures. In every country where these forces have prevailed, there have been massive book burnings, and Syria was no exception.

Because she hadn't any Scriptures to teach her grandson the Word of the Lord, my father's grandmother, Mannah, permitted him to get a job cleaning out latrines, the large holes in the ground which served as public toilets. My dad had to climb into them to clean them out. During this time of persecution, this was the only type of work available to the Jewish youth, no matter how brilliant the boy might have been. My father felt he was very fortunate indeed, because there were really so few jobs available to Jewish boys.

The reason a job was so important to my father was that he knew if there was ever a chance of smuggling in a set of the Scriptures, he was going to need money to pay for them. So every day, with a prayer on his lips, he went to his miserable job. He knew in his heart that the Lord knew what he was working for, and some day, He would answer his prayer.

While he was working in the latrines, my dad was befriended by a young Arab boy near his own age. His name was Abudallah, and he was a true Moslem. Each year his family made a trip to Jerusalem to worship at the Dome of the Rock. This is where Solomon's Holy Temple stood and where the Moslems believe Mohammed and his white steed ascended into heaven.

After much prayer, my father asked Abudallah if he would bring back Scriptures to him when he made his trips. This was really stepping out in faith for my father, because if Abudallah had reported him, his life wouldn't have been worth living. Abudallah had grown to love my dad, and he knew how badly he wanted the Word of God. He knew how much his Koran meant to him. So for the love of a friend, which is God-given, this Moslem boy helped my father become a rabbi.

After he finished his rabbinical training, the family decided that it was time for him to take a wife. It was commanded by God in Leviticus that you are not to marry outside your tribe, and as custom demanded, the family arranged the marriage. After much discussion, with many candidates considered and rejected, they decided upon a young girl of thirteen years named Gilson.

She was a daughter of a second cousin of my father. Her mother's name was Renna Esses, and her father was Rabbi Solomon Antar, who was descended from the royal house of Judah. Gilson was the youngest of twelve children. She was unknown to my father as an individual, since he was twenty-seven years old at the time, and for years she had been just another one of the children playing on the dusty streets. Now, because she had reached puberty, she was of marriageable age and had been selected for my father. The marriage contracts were drawn, the dowry was given, and the couple stood under the canopy and took their vows.

Isaac, now a rabbi with a wife, became well-known to the Judean Jews of Aleppo. At the end of six years, he was the father of five children—four boys, Abood, Samuel, Ezra, Abraham, and one daughter, Garaz. He was also rabbi of the largest congregation of Judean Jews in the area.

All Israelites are Jews, but not all Jews are Israelites. A Judean Jew is a Jew who is of the tribe of Judah. By oral tradition handed down from father to son in our family, even today we know who we are and what tribe we are from. We are all Levites and all are descendants of Aaron, the high priest. Anybody by the name of Levi, Levy, Levinson, or Levinburg is of the tribe of Levi. Anybody by the name of Cohen is a descendant of Aaron, the high priest. The name "Cohen" in Hebrew means "high priest." They have retained their name, so they know who they are and what tribe they are from. Today, in every Orthodox synagogue on the Sabbath, the descendants of Aaron, the high priests, the "cohens," are called forth to stretch out their hands and bless the people of Israel as commanded by God to Moses. Moses told Aaron and all the high priests after him, "It is on this wise you shall bless the people of Israel saying, 'May the Lord bless thee and keep thee. May the Lord let His face shine upon thee and show thee favor. May the Lord lift up His countenance unto thee and give thee peace. Amen.'"

We Judean Jews have always looked down our noses at

our fellow brethren of the people of Israel. We felt we were the aristocrats of the Hebrew people, for after all, didn't God bring forth King David and King Solomon from the tribe of Judah? When our Leah, wife of Jacob the Patriarch, gave birth to Judah, the Holy Spirit descended on her, and the words came forth from her lips: "This time will I praise the Lord." This told us that our Messiah would be coming from the tribe of Judah. This was before God made the promise to King David that from him would come an everlasting kingdom and a King who would personally live forever.

For these reasons, we always felt we were a little better than our fellow Israelites. Consequently, we isolated ourselves, having our own synagogues, our own congregations, and our own merchants. We would neither buy, sell, trade, nor worship with our fellow Israelites. This isolation still persists in this country even today.

This polarization is causing a tremendous problem in Israel. The basic problem is that most Judean Jews stayed in and around the Middle East, and continued to live as in the days of the Bible. Our Israelite brethren migrated to most of the European nations and took on their customs and traditions. They even coined a new language, Yiddish, which is about 90 percent German.

So now we have, on one hand, Judean Jews, people totally steeped in and committed to biblical ways, people who are like the Pharisees of old. They believe in the coming Messiah, the coming resurrection, life hereafter, heaven and hell, and all the many things prophesied in the Bible. They could care less about the preservation of the state, about progress, or any factor that distracts man's mind from God.

On the other hand, we have the European Jew, Jews from Germany, Poland, Czechoslovakia, Lithuania, Russia, etc. These are the most brilliant of all Jews. They are the mathematicians, physicists, doctors, lawyers, or to sum it up, the most highly educated and trained Jews. But the most important thing they are is Zionist. These are the people who fought for and established the state of Israel. They are a modern contemporary people, and most are Reform Jews who have totally rejected the rabbinical laws for which the Judean Jew would die.

What it boils down to is the Zionist Jew feels that he and his have fought to establish this country of Israel; now he wants to govern it as he sees fit. My people have come back to Israel and say that the Zionist didn't establish the land, that it was established in fulfillment of God's Word in Isaiah 66:8, the 37th chapter of Ezekiel, and Isaiah 43 — that it was God who established the land. Therefore, His biblical and rabbinical laws should rule the land.

Result? Complete stalemate.

4

IN 1902, the persecution of the Jews in Syria was extremely severe, and mother and dad were in continual prayer to the Lord for guidance. After much prayer, my folks felt that the Lord was freeing them from this land, and they decided to apply for exit permits. In due time, an exit permit came, and they started rejoicing—until they realized it was for only one person, my father.

The people in authority knew that out of all the applicants for emigration, the one it would most behoove them to be rid of was the head rabbi. He was the one who would most likely keep the people on their religious kick, and maybe without him they would have an easier time controlling these stiff-necked people. Many ask me, "When the Jewish people were so hated, why wouldn't the authorities let them get out of their countries?"

First of all, they were usually doing all the manual labor at miserable wages. Jewish emigration would have been as devastating to their economy as it was to the South when she lost her slaves. Second, there are many brilliant people amongst the Jews, and the countries where they lived didn't want to lose their brain power. Third, the heads of most of these governments needed someone to be their scapegoat, someone to take the blame for all their mistakes.

After much prayer, it was decided that the Lord must have wanted dad to come to America, because his exit permit did come through. With the help of her parents, my mother was to continue applying for permits for herself and the children, and in the meantime, my dad would be making a home for them in America. With the faith of a true believer in God, my father was sure the Lord would not permit his family to be broken up.

So they said their good-byes, and my father left, fully expecting to see his wife and children in a few months. The Lord didn't let my father down, but His timetable was not the same as dad's. It was twenty years before his family joined him on American soil.

When my father left Syria, he had to leave with only the clothes on his back. When he arrived in the United States, his first problem was to make a living. After working for a while at whatever he could scrounge, he was finally able to purchase a pushcart, and he was in business. He joined the thousands of other immigrants on the Lower East Side who began this way in this country.

It's amazing what this man was able to do from such a humble beginning. His goal, a home for his family, was the stimulus that overcame the drawbacks of being a foreigner, not being able to speak the language, and not having any money.

By the time my mother and the family joined him twenty years later, he was rabbi of the largest congregation of Judean Jews in New York. He had a home paid for and waiting for them. He was involved in real estate, owning quite a few stores on one of the business blocks of Brooklyn —quite an achievement for a man who started out cleaning latrines.

During those twenty years, life was an up-and-down affair for my mother and the kids. Sometimes the oppression was very harsh; other times it wasn't so bad. It depended on who happened to be in power in Syria at the time.

A graphic example of the trials to which my family was subjected, happened at the end of the First World War. The German and Turkish armies had arrived at the city of Aleppo in order to kill all its Christians and Jews. There was chaos throughout the town as these helmeted soldiers crashed into the hiding places of Christians and Jews alike. My mother told me that the family had all hidden together at my grandfather's house. Hearing the sounds of the shooting, running, and shouting that filtered down into the cellar from the streets, they felt they were all doomed. They would have been, too, except that the British, who had been waiting for the Germans and Turks to make this move, arrived in time to save most of our people, including my family.

There were times when there were as many as twenty people living like cattle in caves under the house. At other times, they were able to stay in homes like civilized people.

Since my father was not permitted to send any money from America, it was up to my mother's father to take over the burden of supporting the family. It was not easy for him, but he did it with no complaints. He felt it was his duty until my father was permitted to do it or until the boys were old enough to take over.

When the children were still small, they used to collect used lead bullets that were scattered all over the country of Syria. They sold the lead, which was melted down and re-used. This helped a lot with the support of the family.

There were many times during those years when the children could have used their father at home. The boys were lively and needed a man to control them. One day the youngest son, Abraham, made a terrible mistake. There were two similar kegs on one of the shelves in the house. One of them had a clear white liquid named arrack, a

180-proof liquor made from raisins and anise seeds. My mother used to give it to the boys for teething discomfort, for a bellyache, and a variety of other ailments. Well, Abraham thought it would be a good idea to take a drink of this arrack. Instead, he got a stomach full of the white gasoline that was in the other keg. This caused him trouble for the rest of his life, and was eventually the cause of his death.

It was hard to keep the boys in line, especially Abraham. He was always getting into fights with the Moslem boys. He was very small for his age, and about as cocky as they come. So many times, the small boys are the ones always in trouble. Abraham would get into fights, and Ezra would have to wade in and finish them. Ezra was as strong as a young bull, and not many of the Arab boys could lick him — even the ones who were years older. And so, even though Ezra was next to the youngest, he became the father of the family.

Eventually, Syria became mandated to France, and my father was notified that his family would be allowed to leave and immigrate to the United States. He had to contact the Department of Immigration, put up a bond guaranteeing their passage, and also guaranteeing that he would be financially responsible for them. With a thankful heart, he complied with all the requirements.

My mother was informed that all the arrangements had been made, so the family began to get ready to go. There were many good-byes to be said and promises that the rest of the family would follow. Abood and Samuel were both engaged, Abood to a neighbor girl, and Samuel to his first cousin. The boys promised to return for the girls as soon as possible.

When it came time to leave for the United States, my people were placed upon the boat and tagged with a red tag that was to be worn until they passed through Immigration in America. For some reason, this infuriated Ezra. For years he talked about that red tag. It was a point of humiliation for him, and he never forgave them for making him wear it.

5

MY MOTHER and the family, now five adults, arrived in New York in the spring of 1922. It's hard to imagine what they must have been thinking as the ship slipped into the harbor. They hadn't been able to tell my father when they would arrive, so they knew no one would be at the dock to meet them. They had been on the high seas for several weeks, assailed by a whole gamut of emotions.

My mother wondered what my father would be like after twenty years—if he would even recognize her, since she was a twenty-year-old girl when he left, and now she was a forty-year-old woman. Her heart was pounding so hard she was afraid it would burst. She was tired, scared, and very close to tears, as the landing was made.

My brothers' and sister's emotions were mainly apprehensive. Only Abood and Samuel could even vaguely remember my father; the others didn't remember him at all. They had kept asking my mother about him all during the trip, trying in vain to picture him in their minds. She was really not much help, because Isaac had become too remote even for her memory. This was a moment they had talked about, planned on, and waited for for twenty years, and now that it was here, they all wished it was still in the future.

18

Of all the seasons of the year, spring is the time when New York is at her best. Her trees are full of fresh foliage. Her flowers are in bloom. The ladies are resplendent in their beautiful spring hats. The dispositions of her people are at their best, as they are happy and grateful that the sloppy, slushy winter has bid adieu, and lovely spring has made her entrance. My family felt America was giving them a glorious welcome when it laid New York at their feet.

The only cloud on their horizon was the forthcoming confrontation with my father. It was after some difficulty that they finally located him, in a section of Brooklyn you could safely call "little Syria." This was an area where the Judean Jews were separate from the people of Israel. We were hemmed in on one side by the Irish Catholics and on the other side by the Italians.

The meeting with my father proved the validity of the apprehensions with which my brothers and sister had been burdened. He was a true patriarch, in every sense of the word. The boys, especially, had been on their own since they were little children. They felt they were very much men, and now they were faced with a man none of them knew, who expected them to be totally subservient to him. Their father expected to be held in complete honor and esteem, with his every utterance, law. They were to kiss his hand and make obeisance to him.

The only one of the boys who fulfilled what his father expected of him was Ezra. He and his father were very much alike, and as unlikely as it seems, with two such strong personalities, these two had a special affinity for each other. For the other boys, it was the start of a lifetime struggle to come to terms with their father. This conflict was probably the reason Abood and Samuel left shortly for Syria to bring back their brides and set up their own households.

It would be hard to say what my mother felt. She was a

woman who had been brought up in the old-world tradition that her sole function was to serve her husband and children. There seemed to be a total acceptance of her lot in life. She fulfilled with graciousness the role of a rabbi's wife, and was very dear to the members of my father's congregation. In these days of woman's lib, it's hard to imagine a woman as content with life as she was.

To understand the complete control my father had over his family, you have to understand the role he played in their lives. In order to immigrate to this country, you had to have a sponsor. My father sponsored approximately twenty relatives, and from the beginning of his sponsorship, he was patriarch of the whole clan and all their offspring.

One example of the patriarch in action involved my sister Garaz. For some reason that I do not know, she had never married. She was a beautiful woman, who at the age of thirty-five was working as a designer of wedding dresses, but had never worn one of her own. I don't know how she met him, but she started to see a non-Jewish man who was a doctor. They fell in love and wanted to be married. When my father was apprised of this fact, he put his foot down and completely forbade my sister to even see this man again.

This unfortunate love affair galvanized my father into action. Within a few short weeks, he had looked over the eligible men in our community, selected one, signed the marriage contracts, given the dowry, and informed my sister of her fate — all strictly according to Jewish law. This proved to be a very bad match for my sister, but she always said, "My father made my bed, and I will lie in it."

6

NEW YORK, New York, that wonderful town. Our 747 is now in a holding pattern over my hometown. I look over that marvelous skyline as we come in from the sea, and I'm flooded with memories, both good and bad.

I can remember the complete loyalty my father had to this country. He felt he was the most fortunate of men to be allowed to live here. There was never a moment that he was in this country that he thought about or even considered visiting the old country. You hear many people of foreign birth talk about how wonderful the old country was, no matter how miserable it had been for them when they lived there. As far as my father was concerned, there was only one country, America.

It was really a wonderful day for my dad when his first American son was born. It was on April 28, 1923, that I came into the world. I was born at home, just as I would have been if I had been born in the old country. I doubt if it ever even entered my mother's mind to go to the hospital.

On the eighth day of my life, I was circumcised, and my name was written in the rolls of the Book of Life of Israel. By being circumcised on the eighth day as commanded by God to Abraham, I became a Son of the Covenant and entered into a covenant relationship with God. This event is called a *berith* in Hebrew. It is also known as a *briss*. It is a big affair, with all the family and friends attending. There is a huge spread of food, and many presents for the baby.

The circumcision of a Jewish child follows a very rigid and set formula. It is customary for all those witnessing a circumcision to remain standing, for it is written in II Kings 23:3, "And all the people stood to the covenant." There are two chairs; one is for the man who has been chosen to be godfather. He sits in the chair and holds the child. The other is the chair for Elijah. This tradition comes from Malachi, chapter three, where Elijah was called the Messenger or Angel of the Covenant. At every Passover, and at every circumcision, there is a place set aside for Elijah.

When the circumcision has been performed, the father gives a benediction, and those assembled say, "Just as he has been initiated into the covenant, so may he be initiated into the study of the Torah, to his nuptial canopy, and to the performance of good deeds."

7

WHEN I look back at my childhood, it is very painful to me, even now that I am a man. Unconsciously, we all think a child should be at least reasonably happy, but searching through my memory as hard as I can, I can't come up with even one happy moment. It was a life of total restriction by my father and total rebellion by me — not the kind of rebellion you see nowadays, with unhappy kids turning to drugs to find that euphoric state they long for, but the subtle kind of rebellion that shows the underlying rage that a child has for a way of life he feels is totally unfair.

I was quite small, no more than two, when I had already established the vicious circle my life was to become. I was obnoxious and mean because I wasn't welcome among family and friends, and I wasn't welcome because I was obnoxious and mean.

It's hard to pinpoint the beginning, but I imagine it started with the birth of my kid brother, David. You would think that I would have been overjoyed with this event, but the single most important thing it meant to me was that I was put out of my mother's bed. Until David's birth, I slept with my mother and was very possessive of her. I was probably very special to her, a baby after so many years, but with a new baby arriving on the scene, I wasn't that special anymore, and mother's time and love had to be divided between us. So, the reign of terror began.

It soon became impossible for mother to take me to the homes of any of our relatives or friends, because I was so destructive. There would be oil turned over in the kitchens, children and animals teased, temper tantrums thrown — by a defiant little boy who still wanted his mother to love him more than anyone else in the world.

I can remember one incident which involved some kittens. It was the birthday of one of my cousins, and I wanted to go to the party. The only problem was that my aunt had called and begged my mother not to bring me. My mother agreed. Now she had the problem of breaking the news to me. As kindly as possible, she told me that I couldn't go, but that she would stay at home with me.

If she had released a full-blown hurricane, she couldn't have had a more violent reaction than she got from me. I simply went wild. After a bout of completely uncontrollable screaming and kicking, I topped the whole thing off by climbing on the top of the house and throwing the kittens off the roof.

My father came home at about this point, and I found myself across his knee with his belt being applied to my backside. When he was finished, my dad gave me a talk on cruelty to animals, and what God had to say on the subject in Leviticus. Well, I was in no mood for a sermon, so I finished off my day by going up on the roof again. This time, instead of throwing the kittens off, I threw myself off. The immediate result was a broken nose. My father asked me, first, to repent for what I had done, and then, he said, he would take me to the doctor. Needless to say, I refused, and this day left a lasting impression upon me — right in the middle of my face.

It was about this time that I began Hebrew school. Because I was the first son my father would help to raise, it was expected that I would follow in his footsteps and become a rabbi. I was fortunate enough to have a very retentive mind, so my folks knew I had the ability to achieve, even if I didn't have the desire. About the last place I wanted to be was in Hebrew school, but one morning bright and early, complete with a Little Lord Fauntleroy velvet suit, I appeared in Hebrew school.

This new environment with its rigorous discipline was just as bad as I expected it to be. You were rapped repeatedly on the knuckles if you didn't pay attention, and the strap was used when you didn't know your lessons.

The method of teaching was to go through the Pentateuch, the first five books of the Old Testament, verse by verse. We expounded each verse literally, then debated its meaning over and over until a conclusion was formed. By the age of five, we were expected to know each verse, and if called upon, to explain its exact meaning.

With the advent of Hebrew school came the advent of the every-morning bout of the manhole cover. Each morning would find me sent out the door, beautifully dressed for Hebrew school, and each morning would find me also lying out in the middle of the street on the manhole cover. I would lie there waiting for a car to run over me, knowing that my mother, watching me from the doorway, would soon be hysterical. I got the attention I wanted, even if it cost me a spanking from my father, who would arrive after a frantic call from my mother.

My father then walked me to Hebrew school, lecturing me every inch of the way about my duty to my father and to God. I was told that the Word of the Lord came before anything else, and that my rebellious nature was separating me from God. I was also usually given a dose of castor oil, as a form of discipline, when we arrived at the school.

At the age of five, through much discipline and prayer by

my mother and father, and an *awful* lot of castor oil, I did know the entire Pentateuch.

At the age of six, I suddenly had another big problem in my life – public school. I, of course, had been told this was coming, but I didn't want to think about it. My biggest difficulty was that I couldn't speak any English. I spoke only Hebrew, Arabic, Aramaic, and Chaldean, even though I was born in America.

Unless you are a child of immigrants, as I was, you have no idea how cloistered you can be in a big city like New York. My family rarely ventured out of our little section of Brooklyn. The main reason they stayed so close to home was because they couldn't speak any English, either. In our little section of Brooklyn, the butcher, the baker, and the candlestick maker were all Syrian Jews, so they felt very much at home.

When the day dawned on which I was to begin public school, my sister Garaz (now Grace) was the lucky person elected to get me enrolled, because she knew a little English. After the day I put her through, I imagine she wished she was still as ignorant about the language as my parents were.

In the first place, I wasn't about to go, so every threat this side of death was used to get me moving. After they invoked the name of the Lord, I finally moved out, but with great reluctance. There were many mistakes made that day – innocent mistakes, but mistakes just the same – that left lasting effects on me.

The first and probably worst mistake was my attire. I was sent in the same Little Lord Fauntleroy suit that I had worn to Hebrew school. These clothes were proper for a little Jewish boy in Hebrew school. In fact, I was the best-dressed boy there, as was befitting my position as the chief rabbi's son. But can you imagine short velvet pants with suspenders, a little blue velvet jacket, white satin shirt, and a beautiful bow tie going to public school? It doesn't take much imagination to know what those Irish and Italian boys had to say when they got a look at me.

It soon became my morning ritual to have a fight with one of those boys before I arrived at my class each day.

I had the misfortune to have for my teacher a Mrs. Kossorsky who was a European Jew, and there was no love lost in her feelings for all Judean Jews. It's a paradox that my first real taste of prejudice would be from a fellow Jew. When I came into class, I was usually in a mess, with clothes all awry, sometimes torn, and always dirty from the fight I had been involved in. Mrs. Kossorsky always said, "Well, here comes King Solomon in all his glory," and then she would make me sit on a stool in front of the class with a dunce hat on my head. These incidents certainly helped solidify the basic rebellion I felt as a child toward all people in authority.

One incident which stands out in my memory was the "Cucumber Caper." Every summer, dad would buy bushels of delicious small cucumbers from which my mother would make kosher pickles. I really looked forward to the appearance of these baskets, as I dearly loved those little baby cucumbers.

It was a particularly warm summer day, close to the end of the public-school year. I came home tired, warm, and hungry. I yelled for my mother as I slammed through the front door, and since I didn't get an answer, I knew she must have gone shopping.

I made my way through the house — school books dropped here, shoes dropped there, lunch box on a chair — doing all the usual things for which a six-year-old will get a scolding. And then I noticed the cellar door was ajar.

"Gee! That's a perfect place to go on a hot day like this, our nice cool cellar." Down I went, and to my surprise, standing in the middle of the floor was a beautiful little basket of cucumbers. There they sat, cool, green, and crisp—the perfect between-school snack for a little boy. (At the time, I attended public school in the forenoon and Hebrew school in the afternoon and evening.) "Gosh, I wish mother was home. I know she would say I could have a cucumber. Well, since I know she would say, 'Have a cucumber,' it would be a shame if I didn't have one. Let's see which one looks like it would taste the best. This one looks good, but maybe I can find one that's a little bigger. Ah, here's one that looks like the largest one here. Mmmm, that was sure good. You know, when I take a look at this basket I can't even tell that cucumber I ate is missing, so it probably wouldn't hurt if I had another one. Boy! Dad outdid himself selecting this basket; these are the best cucumbers I ever had. Maybe just one more . . ." After approximately one-half hour of rationalizing, there was quite a dent made in the cucumbers. In fact, there was just about one-half of the basket gone.

When the realization of what I had done got through to me, my mind went into high gear trying to figure out some story to tell my father and mother. I finally settled on a bad case of mice who were fond of cucumbers.

I got out of the cellar as fast as possible, gathered up my things, so Mom wouldn't know I had ever been home, and took off for Hebrew school. What happened next made me a believer in retribution from that day forward. As I sat in Hebrew school, I got a few twinges in my stomach, which I chalked up to gas from the cucumbers, and I tried to ignore it. It was soon apparent that I wasn't going to be able to ignore anything. I was getting sicker by the moment. I had a bellyache like you wouldn't believe. It had me doubled over in cramps, and I started yelling for a doctor. I knew without a shadow of a doubt that I was about to die, and by then the pain was so bad I was afraid I *wouldn't* die.

My teacher, the rabbi, called my father, and he arrived in a hurry. I think the screaming he could hear in the background, while my teacher made the call, spurred him on. The two men very calmly consulted together about the nature of my illness. Was it appendicitis, a kink in my intestinal tract, ptomaine poisoning, or what? As I listened to these learned men discussing my condition, I couldn't keep quiet any longer. *"It's cucumbers!"* I yelled.

One phone call home to my mother, who quickly checked the cellar and then told my dad the extent of my gluttony, gave my father all the facts he needed. In a very matter-of-fact tone of voice, he told me that he was not going to get the doctor. I had sinned against the Lord, and if I wanted to be healed, I would have to ask the Lord to heal me. I became absolutely furious.

Out the door, screaming like a banshee, I raced, with my father walking calmly behind me. Over and over in my mind went the desire to get even with my father for not showing more pity toward his suffering son. Many ideas flashed through my mind, like one little light bulb after another. "That's it! The light bulb—that will fix him!" By the time my father got home, I had taken a chair, placed it on the kitchen table, climbed up, unscrewed the turned-on light bulb, and with all the assurance of one who has come up with the perfect revenge, I stuck my left thumb into the live empty socket. My mother was in a state of total hysterics when my father walked in the door.

He placidly took in the scene that met his eyes. My mother was screaming louder than I was, and I was standing there shaking and jerking from the electricity going through my body. Boy! Was I getting even! I knew I finally had him on the ropes. He would surely panic and run for a doctor, ask my forgiveness, or at least say he was sorry. No. He calmly walked over, pulled the table and chair out from under me, and said, "Praise the Lord," as I fell to the floor. Then, to my total chagrin, he asked me if I would *now* ask the Lord to forgive me of my sin, and he assured me that if I did, the Lord would heal me. Needless to say, I gave in, and the Lord healed me. The only reminder He left me was a scar on my left thumb that I carry to this day.

8

ONE VERY good result of public school was that it didn't take me long to learn the English language. Right from the first day I was impressed with the need for experience in this area. After the first three hours of school, I had to go to the bathroom. How in the world are you going to ask your teacher if you can go to the bathroom if you don't speak one word of English? First I wiggled and squirmed in my seat, but that worked for only so long. Then I was on my feet, first the left foot, then the right foot. I finally attracted the teacher's attention, but by the time she understood what I wanted, the emergency was all over. At my feet was a puddle that, to my eyes, looked like Lake Erie.

From this point on, whenever my teacher saw me getting at all restless, she always chased me out of the room. This incident was a source of such embarrassment for me that I immediately resolved that with God's help I would learn English, and I would learn it fast.

There is one other thing I feel I should tell about here. This is also a source of embarrassment to me, but it was very much part of my life. Are you ready for this? My baby bottle. I was eight years old when it was finally taken away from me. I have never figured out why my parents let me have it so long. I know it represented security for me, but I had to be so ashamed of it, that I can't see how the security could compensate for the negative side of the situation.

I knew better than to take my bottle to public school, but I took it to Hebrew school daily. I could get away with having it there because of father's position. The incident that finally took it out of my life happened at Hebrew school.

Every evening, our rabbi would send out for apple pie and coffee for himself and his students. This was our reward for lessons well-done, and a much-welcomed break in our day.

On this particular day, I was being punished for some infraction of the rules, and the rabbi decided that it would be good for my character if I were denied the treat of the apple pie and coffee that evening. To say that I didn't care for that decision would be putting it mildly. With very careful aim, I hurled my baby bottle through the Star of David stained-glass window of the synagogue. That was the last of the baby bottle. I guess my parents decided any kid who had the nerve to pull a trick like that was secure enough.

It was during the summer of my ninth year that my father decided to take the family, which then consisted of my parents, my brother David, and myself, to Keansburg, New Jersey, for a two-week holiday. This is the one and only vacation I remember as a child. My father rented a room for us in a boardinghouse on the boardwalk. This was the first time I had ever seen my parents out of their usual environment. The way we lived our lives was such a natural thing, at home, but here it seemed so out of place.

The first thing we did that was different from the people with whom we were living was eating. While everyone else from the boardinghouse sat at the communal table and ate the food prepared by the landlady, our family ate alone in our room. My mother had prepared food, most of it dried, and we ate nothing but this food, in order to preserve our kosher laws. I can remember how good the food downstairs smelled and how I wanted to be eating in that big dining room instead of upstairs in our room.

The second thing that I couldn't get used to was my father's prayers. No matter where he was, when it came time to pray, he would pray. If we were out on the boardwalk, and it was time, he would stop, bow to God, and go into the proper prayer for that moment. At home this was an everyday occurrence, but here among strangers, it became a curiosity, and I really didn't know how to react. I wanted to be loyal to my father and my God, but I was embarrassed among these strangers who would stop and poke each other and point at my father.

I, as a Sephardic Orthodox Jewish child, had been told by my parents that it was a sin to associate with Christian children, that it was a sin to listen to church bells, that it was a sin to walk past a church if it wasn't absolutely necessary. I was told that if I associated with Christians or became friendly with them, they would eat my flesh and drink my blood, because that is what they did with a Jew named Jesus.

Here I was on a vacation, surrounded by the Gentiles I had been warned against, and now *we* were the ones who seemed out of step and different. They seemed to have a better time than we did. They seemed more free and happy within their families than we were. I found myself envying the casual camaraderie I saw between other boys and their fathers. I watched them playing in the surf together, walking arm and arm down the boardwalk together, eating ice cream cones together, laughing on the rides together— These are all things you find hard to do with a patriarch from the old world.

I know now that I was going through that confusing period that all children of immigrants go through when they are being raised in a culture into which their parents have no intention of melding. The Conservative and the Reform Jews have made that transition, but it is a different story with the Sephardic Orthodox Jew. They cling tenaciously to the old customs, and it is really very hard on their American-born children.

During this vacation, I fell madly in love for the first time. Sally was the daughter of some of the other tenants in our boardinghouse, and I thought she was the most beautiful creature I had ever seen. Beautiful blond hair and china blue eyes. How could you beat that combination? After I came back home, we used to write to each other, but when my father found that I was corresponding with a Christian girl, he put a stop to it immediately.

When I started my school year after this summer, I was a different boy inside. I was really starting to question the difference in my childhood and the childhood of my peers in public school. I had to go to public school from eight in the morning until two in the afternoon, then to Hebrew school from two-thirty in the afternoon until ten at night. This was the routine I followed until I graduated from high school.

I never had a pair of roller skates, a bike, a ball or bat, or a birthday party. There was never time for sports, or the neighborhood playtimes that all the other children indulged in. In fact, you might say that I grew up with no childhood whatsoever.

I soon learned that there were some things about school that I just could not tell my parents. One of these things was a period called "assembly," a time set aside for all the classes at school to meet together in the school auditorium. We would sing hymns, and someone would read out of the Old Testament; then someone else would read out of the New Testament. This was climaxed by everyone reciting the Lord's Prayer together.

Assembly was my favorite part of the day, and I always looked forward to it. If my parents had known about assembly and what I was being exposed to, I would have been pulled out of public school immediately.

One of the most vivid memories of my childhood was the yearly ritual of the Day of Atonement. God told Moses that the Hebrew people would have to afflict their souls and atone for their sins once a year, while the high priest went into the holy of holies to make the sacrifice necessary to accomplish this atonement. The high priest sacrified a burnt offering, a sin offering, and a peace offering to the Lord. Then he laid his hands on a live goat and transmitted all the sins of the people of Israel to the *scape goat*. The goat was then sent into the wilderness, carrying all our iniquities with it.

Later, a new sacrificial system came into existence to replace the old. In the 613 rabbinical laws, it states that we are to sacrifice a hen for the mother of the family, a pullet for any unmarried girl, a rooster for the father, and a young cock for the unmarried males of the family. This was done by cutting the jugular vein, bringing a great effusion of blood and quick unconsciousness.

Each member of the family then laid hands on his chicken, transmitting his sins to the chicken. My mother plucked the chickens, roasted them, and each of us ate his own sacrifice on the evening of the Day of Atonement.

Then we went to the synagogue to be baptized with water for the remission of our sins. We repented and asked forgiveness of the Lord and afflicted our souls by fasting until the next night at sundown.

My father used to perform the ritual of cutting the chickens' throats down in our cellar, and as his eldest boy at home, it was my job to help him. To say that I looked upon this occasion with dread would be the understatement of the year. For many nights preceding, I had nightmares, and my days were filled with anguish because of the coming event.

Finally the Day of Atonement would be upon me. My father would lead me downstairs, and I would lay the live chicken in his lap for him to say the prayer over. After the prayer, he would take the knife and cut the chicken's throat. The chickens were supposed to die quickly, but it seemed to me that they took forever.

The explosive sound of cackling, to my ears, sounded like screams that reached a horrible crescendo. The chickens always escaped from my father's hands, and the wild whooshing sounds as they flew around the room splattering blood on everything and everybody was too much for my mind to bear. I would feel the walls of the cellar closing in on me as the volume and intensity of those ungodly sounds increased. By the time the death throes of one chicken were over, it was time to sacrifice the next one.

Every year would find me being led up out of the cellar in a state of shock. My mother would then take over, helping to clean me up and giving me the TLC I needed at this time. I would soon be filled with a sense of relief that another year would pass before I would have to go through this ordeal again. Praise God.

When the morning dawned on my thirteenth birthday, I felt that my life would surely change, for this was the day I would stand before God and the congregation and become a Bar Mitzvah. I would no longer be a child. I would become a man in Israel. This was the day when I would re-affirm the vows that were taken for me by my father on the day of my circumcision, when my name was written in the rolls of the Book of Life of Israel.

A wonderful celebration party was being readied for me. My mother had been cooking and baking for days. Even my father was in a joyous mood. He had been praising the

Lord more fervently each day as each day brought him closer to liberation. By Hebrew tradition, my father had been held responsible for all my sins until I became thirteen. Now the Lord was starting a new sheet with just my name on it, and I would be held responsible from this day forward. I would now become a Son of the Law. My dad truly praised the Lord, because he figured he was finally free.

Six months before my thirteenth birthday, I had been re-dedicated and consecrated to the Lord in preparation for this day. Now it was here, and I was so excited. How do I describe to you what was probably the biggest event of the day, a happening that I had looked forward to for ages, one which I was sure would take me from the wretched state of little boy to the wonderful existence of a MAN— my first long pants? Oh! How beautiful I looked, how grown up, how sophisticated. When I stood in front of the mirror with my new suit, new shirt, new tie, new shoes— everything new—I looked brand-new also. I was so proud, and I went through the rest of the day with a new sense of dignity.

All of my family had arrived to go to the synagogue for the ceremony. As I came downstairs, they all exclaimed about how grown up and handsome I looked. My father and mother looked very proud, and I knew they were hoping I would do them honor during the ceremony that was about to be performed.

I was given the Ark of the Torah from which to read the Scripture I had selected; then I proceeded to address the congregation. I was to tell the rabbis, the elders, and the people what this day meant to me. I don't remember much of what I said, but I do remember my closing line, "That I would follow in the footsteps of my forefathers and illuminate the word of God to His people."

During my Bar Mitzvah, I was given my first prayer

shawl (fringes) and my first set of phylacteries. Every Orthodox Jew wears the prayer shawl under his clothes all day long. Every time he looks upon this garment, he is to be reminded of the 613 laws that were given to the Jewish people (Num. 15:39).

The phylacteries are small leather cases with leather straps attached to them. Enclosed in the cases are the Scriptures, Exodus 13:1-10,11-16 and Deuteronomy 6:4-9; 11:13-21. These four sections have been chosen in preference to all other passages of the Old Testament because they embrace the acceptance of the kingdom of heaven, the unity of the Creator, and the exodus from Egypt. These are the fundamental doctrines of Judaism.

All my life I had watched my father place the phylacteries on his head and his left arm during his morning prayers. I had been taught the beautiful reason that God had given for this observance, so I looked forward to the time when I could wear phylacteries, too. My dad had told me that you place them on your left arm, opposite the heart, as a memorial to God's outstretched arm, to indicate the duty of subjecting the longings and designs of our heart to His service. God commanded us also to put the phylacteries on our heads against the brain, thereby teaching that the mind, whose seat is in the brain, together with all senses and faculties, is to be subjected to His service.

As the prayer shawl was placed on my shoulders, and I was shown how to wrap the leather straps from the phylacteries on my left arm in the prescribed manner, it was as if the traditions and obligations of all my forefathers were now being placed in my hands. I could feel the tears in my eyes start to roll down my cheeks, and I was soon weeping unashamedly in front of the entire congregation. I was a man in the Lord's eyes.

9

KENNEDY AIRPORT. It's been twenty years since I've been to New York. I expected to be hit by waves of nostalgia as soon as I put my foot on New York turf. But Kennedy seems like just one more airport; I might as well be back in Los Angeles.

Then I realize it's not the city itself that will put me in touch with my youth again, it's the people. It's the people who make up the complexion of any city. It's the people who make New York different from Los Angeles, or Chicago, or Seattle.

Here, indeed, is the melting pot of the United States. In any given commercial block of New York City you will probably find a representative from every country of the world. I will thank God the rest of my life because my father decided to join the rest of these immigrants who have come to this country for the better life.

We have a three-hour layover here, so I decide to take my wife for a cab ride through my hometown. The city has changed so much that I have a hard time pointing out many landmarks to her. As we near the district of Brooklyn where I lived as a child, the surroundings begin to look much more familiar. We pass the grade school I attended,

then, down a couple of blocks, the house where I was born
and raised. It looks small to me now. I always thought of it
as a huge house, the very center of my existence. Now it
just looks like one more of the small wooden houses with
very little yard in which a child could play. Further down
the street is the unostentatious synagogue with the adja-
cent yeshiva (Jewish seminary) where I spent so many of
my teenage years.

This humble place has more memories than any other
I've seen. I can still see myself as a youth coming here
after my stint of public school was over for the day. Here
we would memorize, talk, and debate over the Scriptures.
I would much rather, as I walked in the door, have been
playing stick ball with the other kids, but the Lord had a
way of grabbing my attention. I would soon be immersed
in thoughts and words that held me spellbound.

Our teacher was a mild-mannered rabbi about forty years
of age. He always wore the traditional black coat, black hat,
beard, and earlocks (a single long curl at each ear). When
he wasn't teaching, he was a quiet, self-effacing man. If it
were not for his manner of dress, you would have never
given him a second thought. Yet when he started teaching
God's Word, something miraculous happened. The words
and thoughts that were written thousands of years before
became alive, and as relevant as if they had been given
this day. The rabbi's love for the Scriptures was poured
out upon all his students.

Seeing the yeshiva again made me remember the many
evenings, that stretched into years, that I spent in this
dimly lit schoolhouse. I might as well have been in the old
country, a thousand years ago, because the same method
of teaching was used in my time as was used in those by-
gone years. There were no visual aids, no videotapes, not
even a blackboard and some chalk—just a dedicated rabbi

and the ancient Hebrew books that my father and all my ancestors before him had used in order to become rabbis.

There was the Talmud, the writings constituting the body of early Jewish civil and religious law. These consisted of 248 positive commandments and 365 negative commandments. Oh, how I remember the debates we had over these! Then there was the Midrash, ten books that were an interpretation of the scriptural text, usually in homiletic fashion. It took years to consume these text by text.

We went through the Mishnah, a collection of the statements, discussions, and biblical interpretations of many ancient rabbis and sages; the Pentateuch with Rabbi Rashi's commentary; and the Zohar which is the fundamental work of Spanish caballa, taking the form of a commentary on the Pentateuch and a textbook on Jewish medieval mysticism.

These were some of the many books I devoured chapter by chapter, verse by verse, until I was able to hold my own in discussing these works with the best of scholars. We lived and breathed the Scriptures until they became part of our being.

During those years when I was being so steeped in God's words, my life was often a paradox. On one hand, I was the young man who loved God with all his heart and wanted to serve Him for the rest of his life, but on the other hand, I was the boy who was still so rebellious it was very hard for him to fit himself into the niche everyone expected him to fill.

Many events during my teenage years contributed to my confusion about who I was and where I was going.

I started these years off with a bang by contracting rheumatic fever when I was fourteen years old. At first I was placed in Mount Sinai Hospital. I think it was my experience in Mount Sinai that put the dread of hospitals in me that I still fight even today.

I had my second experience with racial prejudice in this hospital. My father and brother Ezra (now Eddie) had come to visit me, and after talking and praying with me for a while, they were about to leave when my father tripped and fell against the man in the next bed. The man made an extremely obscene remark about the Jews and about my father in particular. The room was immediately in chaos, because Eddie had his hands around the man's neck, and it took my dad and two nurses to pull him off. The man threatened to sue if he ever saw any of us again, so I was taken home for the rest of my convalescence.

It was a hard six months for me. I would get so tired of lying in my bed. Everyone in the household got their share of my begging them to give me some attention. The one who was the greatest comfort during this time was my kid brother, David. Over the years, after I had gotten over my jealousy of him, David and I had become fast friends.

David was the kind of boy everyone liked. He was extremely kind, and completely unselfish. In fact, he was generous to a fault. Any spending money I got my hands on was instantly gone; then David would share his with me. Whereas everyone else in my family treated me like a kid, to David I was big brother, and he looked up to me as the smartest, toughest, most remarkable big brother anyone ever had. I ate this adoration up with a spoon.

I know there were many times I hurt David when I refused to take him along on some of my escapades. My cousin Sammy, who was a couple of years older than I was, used to play hooky from school with me, and we had all kinds of adventures. We did typical New York kid things, like sneaking into the subway and the movie theaters downtown.

One Saturday afternoon, when Sammy and I should have remained in the synagogue, the elders got into an extremely long-winded discussion about one of the verses in

Genesis. The two of us took advantage of the fact that the men, our fathers included, were so occupied, and we sneaked out. Once again, retribution marched in the door. Sammy and I were fooling around, boxing with each other. It had started off as a friendly bout between cousins, but slowly the blows were landing a little bit harder every time. Suddenly Sammy got in a perfect punch, right on my nose. I saw stars first, but then I saw red. I was in a state of total rage. Hastily looking around, I spied an old oilcan lying in the gutter. Before anyone, including me, knew it, I had grabbed the can and gashed Sammy's cheek wide open with it. As soon as I realized what I had done, I was horrified, but that didn't help the situation much. It took eighteen stitches to close the wound, and Sammy still carries the scar on his face.

I have noticed a peculiar trait in human beings. The more wrong they are, the more they defend what they have done. This was the position I now found myself in. My dad was ready to kill me, but what he kept telling me was, "Repent for what you have done, and ask for forgiveness." I stubbornly refused, so my father took me down in the cellar and locked me in the dark. Since I refused to ask for forgiveness, he left me down there all night. It was so dark in that cellar, I felt I could grab a handful of the blackness. I was literally terrified, but I still wouldn't bend.

The next morning my brother Abraham (Al) came down to get me. To him had been delegated the job of giving me a good beating, since I refused to repent. Of all my brothers, there was only one other rebel, and that was Al. I knew the Lord had put me into understanding hands. Al took me upstairs, closed the bedroom door, removed his belt, and nearly beat the bed to death — while I screamed bloody murder.

When I look back at the many experiences I had with my father where I was really very wrong, I can see a pattern that he always followed that turned me away from God instead of toward God. It seems to me that you should wait until the extreme emotional state that the culprit is experiencing has subsided before you talk to him about repentance. It's hard to ask forgiveness when you're still defending yourself, no matter how wrong you happen to be. Everyone cools down in a matter of time; then you can talk to him about the forgiveness of God. God now becomes his friend instead of one more person to resist.

On the drive back to the airport, I told my wife what it was like to be a high school student, a rabbinical student, and a part-time employee all my latter teen years. Most of the time I felt like a squirrel on a revolving wheel. I think the only thing that saved my sanity was the weekends. Saturday was good because there was no public school, and I didn't have to work, and Sunday was even better, because there was no public school, no shul (synagogue), and no work. The weekdays were something else again.

My day began at sunrise. All Jews are to worship God at sunrise, because Abraham got up at sunrise, in order to obey God's commandment concerning the sacrifice of his son Isaac. Believe me, on some of those cold New York mornings, it was some sacrifice to be obedient to this law. I used to envy those guys who were still in their snug beds while I was jumping up and down to keep from freezing to death.

Next on my agenda was high school. I would usually do my homework between morning worship and the start of my school day. My father insisted that I maintain a good average in high school as well as the yeshiva, mainly because of his position, but also so no one could say a Jewish boy wasn't smart.

I didn't have too much enthusiasm for high school, because there was never time for any of the extracurricular activities that make high school the warm well-remembered time that it should be. Also, because it was known that I was a rabbinical student, I was an object of curiosity. Neither my family nor I ever considered that such frivolities as proms, football games, basketball games, etc., were for me. I was in school strictly for an education—nothing else.

The high-school years are also the years when most young people start to try their wings with the opposite sex. This experimentation was also denied me, because my father had let me know that when it was time, my family would arrange for a bride who would be acceptable to them and also to the community as a rabbi's wife. They had pretty much settled on my cousin Renee, with whom I had grown up, but Renee fell very much in love with another boy, and her father, who loved her dearly, allowed her to marry him.

When my day at high school was finished, I would rush home, where my mother would have a hot meal for me to eat before I left for the yeshiva. This was the best time of the day for me. I loved my mother dearly, and this was usually the only time of the day when I would see her. Ever since I was a little boy, I felt she and David were the only ones who truly loved me, and it was nice to just sit at the kitchen table with her and tell her about some of my pent-up emotions. She knew how unhappy I was with the regimented life I had always led, and even though there was nothing she could do about it, she did give me love and sympathy. She represented the only softness and give in my life. She was the typical Jewish mother who loved in spite of everything, and I in turn loved her.

My hours at the yeshiva were from five to ten. This is where I felt I belonged. Because I was my father's son and also a good student, I was held in some esteem in this school. Whereas in high school I was an oddball, and many

times an object of ridicule, at the yeshiva I became someone. Here I wasn't different. I was a student who was
looked up to, one to whom the other boys came for help
when they didn't have an answer. In my last couple of
years at the yeshiva, I taught nearly as much as I learned.

A short subway ride took me to the warehouse where I
had my part-time job every evening. On the way to work, I
ate the sack lunch my mother had prepared for me. I
punched in about 10:30, and I worked till 1:00. I worked
at this job of packing and shipping for about three years,
until I graduated from high school.

It wasn't much of a job, but it was all that was available
with the limited number of hours that I could work. I had
to have a job, because my father said that after I was Bar-
Mitzvahed, I was a man and had to earn my own way. Half
of what I made, I paid to my father for room and board.

My father said this was the way I would learn responsibility, also, that neither he nor the world owed me a living.
I was to learn to depend solely and entirely on the Lord
and what I could do through Him. I resented it, but I
learned it. I didn't like it, I murmured. I complained. I
griped, but I learned it. I often used to wonder why my
life was so different from that of the other kids I knew,
especially the Gentile kids. They had toys as children,
bikes, vacation, time for play after school — all the things
I was told weren't important but that I longed for. For
most of my teenage years, I was sorry I was a Jewish boy.

Life is very strange. It seems to go along for so long at
a regular clip. You do just about the same thing every day.
You know what to expect from the people around you, and
they know what to expect from you. Then one day it all
changes. In April of 1940, my life was turned upside down.

My mother had never been really strong, but she had
been feeling much worse lately. I knew my family was
worried about her, but nothing much was ever said to me

about how ill she really was. I would ask, but was put off with an answer like, "Oh, she'll feel better in a few days." I was so busy myself that I wasn't nearly as observant as I should have been.

On April 27, the day before my birthday, I came home from high school to find the doctor with my mother. I went in and talked with her, and the only thing that was on her mind was that there was nothing for me to eat. She told me what to fix for myself in the kitchen, and to come and kiss her good-bye before I left for the yeshiva. I did as she told me, and when I went back in the bedroom, mother said that my brother Al might come over. He would need my bed, so she wanted me to stay over at my cousin Sammy's after I got off work. I said okay, that I loved her and wanted her to hurry up and get well. Then I was off to the yeshiva.

The next morning when I woke up, my aunt said that David was at the door, and he wanted to see me. David's face was a total blank. There were tears running down his cheeks. Very quietly he said, "Happy Birthday. Your Mother's dead."

It couldn't be. Things like this didn't happen. It was a joke. A dirty, rotten, cruel joke. I shoved David aside and was out the door running home as fast as I could. I stumbled up the steps with tear-filled eyes that couldn't see, and shaking hands that couldn't open the door.

My father met me, and one look at his face told me it was true. Here was a broken man. Here was a man who was unyielding and as tough as they come, but now he was crying. Crying because he had lost the only person he had ever loved in his entire life. This was the only moment that I felt close to my father in all the years he lived.

The death of my mother left me with a terrible mental conflict. I was completely devastated by my loss, but my grief was selfish. I cared only about what it was doing to me. I didn't care about my father or David or anybody. In fact, it ended with my not even caring about my mother. She had been my only ally in this world, and she had deserted me. I hated her for it.

"Home" is a beautiful word, a word that evokes the picture of stability, a sanctuary, a place of warmth and understanding. A place where you don't have to be perfect to be accepted. A refuge where you can go when the battle of life is too much for you. Where you know you'll be picked up, brushed off, and sent out to face the world again, a bigger and better person.

Unfortunately, there is one essential ingredient—a wife if you are a man, a mother if you are a child. If this person is missing, the home becomes a house, a place to be avoided because it hurts too much to be there.

My father had lived alone for so many years when he was a young man and my mother was still in Syria, that he knew how to fend for himself. He knew how to cook and keep the house, but *then* he was able to anticipate the time when she would be there to care for him. Now there was nothing for him to look forward to except the marriage of his last two sons and eventually a small back room in someone else's home.

It was like seeing one of our gigantic California redwoods toppled to the ground. No longer tall and proud. No longer patriarch of a family. No longer the man everyone came to for advice and counsel. It's surprising how soon people start ferreting out our weaknesses when they start to show, and then begin to slowly turn their backs on the one they used to revere.

A sense of duty brought me home each afternoon to eat with my father and David. My dad would prepare the meal with care, trying desperately to keep us together in some semblance of a family. It was extra hard on holidays or the evening of the Sabbath. By Hebrew law, the wife of the family always lit the Sabbath candles. Now David and I had to watch our father perform this ceremony.

What used to be a ceremony of beauty and awe became torture for us all. To a Jew, it is meritorious to light as many candles as possible to usher in the Sabbath, so my father and mother always had a candelabrum that held nine candles. Now my father laboriously lit each candle with trembling hands and eyes filled with tears of anguish. It seemed to David and me that we had to re-live the death of our mother weekly. The benediction that my father would give, thanking God for the day, tore at our hearts mercilessly.

The rabbis I had studied with at the yeshiva had explained that with the death of Sarah, the blessings which had attended the household of the patriarch Abraham, and the pious customs which distinguished it, came to an end. I was seeing the same phenomenon in my own home.

With the end of the school year and summer upon me, my life changed course again. My uncle and aunt asked me to go with them to Ocean City, New Jersey, where they had a gift shop on the boardwalk. They said they would teach me to sell, and that it would be good for me to get away from the house and my father, at least for the summer. This sounded wonderful to me, as I was more than ready to spread my wings. I knew I would have to have a summer job, and now here was one being handed to me with the added attraction of being out of town. I approached my dad with the idea, and, lo and behold, I received his approval.

This summer opened up a completely different world. My life up to this point had been fairly cloistered and to say I was naïve would have been a gross understatement.

I was in Ocean City only about a month when my brother

Eddie came to visit and asked me to spend the rest of the summer with him and his wife, Helen, in Cincinnati. In Cincinnati, I sowed some wild oats.

Until this time, I had never even had a date with a girl, but I really made up for lost time during those two months. I was like a small child let loose in a candy factory. I was immediately involved with four different women — two that worked for Eddie, and a mother and daughter to whom a friend introduced me. It was a good thing that summer was soon over and I had to get back to New York. I don't think Eddie ever forgave me for the mess he and Helen had to straighten out after I left. It's not easy to pacify two girls who think they are engaged and one who thinks she's pregnant.

When I got back home, I knew I had had a close call with totaling out my life, and this time without any prompting from my father, I repented and asked for forgiveness.

I was soon back in the routine of life that I had followed for the last few years — my senior year at high school, the yeshiva, and a night job. The only thing that was different was my mother's not being there to care for and comfort me. My dad, David, and I had each made his own inadequate adjustments, and we lived together for the next year in a sterile atmosphere, each trying to do right by the other.

Then, on December 7, 1941, the Japanese bombed Pearl Harbor. America was at war. The next day, I enlisted in the Army Air Corps.

There was only one drawback. I was told that I must have my father's signature before I could be accepted for the service. I knew my father would never consent to my enlistment, so I decided to get him to sign the papers without knowing what he was signing. This could be accomplished, because my father never learned to read or write English.

I told my dad that the yeshiva was going on a retreat to

the Catskill Mountains in Upperstate New York, and I needed his signature to go. Later, when my enlistment was a completed fact, and I was ready to leave for the service, I had to tell him what I had done. I asked his forgiveness for betraying him and begged him to give me his blessing.

My father seemed to grow in stature right before my eyes when he said, "Son, you didn't have to trick me. I'm proud you want to serve this country. God knows it's been good to us." Then he put his hands on my head and gave me his benediction:

> May the Lord bless thee and keep thee.
> May the Lord let His face shine upon thee,
>   and show thee favor.
> May the Lord lift up His countenance unto
>   thee and give thee peace. Amen.

10

IN SPITE OF the fact that I enlisted right at the beginning of the war, my time in the Air Corps was singularly uneventful. Time after time, buddies that I met and grew fond of were sent overseas, some never to return. But it seemed that from the beginning of my enlistment, I was being protected all the way.

I was sent first to Miami, Florida, for basic training. This consisted of my staying in one of Miami's finest hotels and taking my training on a three-million-dollar golf course. After completing basic training, I boarded a train, destination Scott Field, Illinois.

I arrived Wednesday afternoon, and by Wednesday evening my buddy, Jack Goldburg, and I had found out that the name of the commander of the base was Major Oscar Ralls. Through a friend who had arrived a couple of weeks before us, two passes were liberated. I filled our names in on the blank passes, traced Major Ralls' signature on them, and Jack and I had passes to go off the base at any hour of the day or night. One thing has to be remembered about this time. The service was in a total turmoil, because, all of a sudden, we were at war, and thousands of men were having to be processed as fast as possible. I would hate to think what would happen to us for pulling the same trick now.

I was immediately assigned to radio operator school. When it became obvious that I would probably never be able to do much more with a radio than to turn it off and on, I was switched to gunnery school.

I surprised myself as well as my instructors by becoming one of the best men they had. I ended up staying right at Scott Field as a gunnery instructor, training other guys so they could go overseas.

I had been in service for over three years when I became very ill with double pneumonia. After nearly four months of my being in the hospital, then out, then back in the hospital, I was given a medical discharge.

I had grown very fond of the service. After all my years of regimentation at home, the routine of the service didn't bother me at all. After all, I was free every night, and that was a lot more than I could say about home. Consequently, I fought the medical board down the line. I wanted to stay in; in fact, I told them I had just about made up my mind to make the service my career. All my pleading was to no avail, however, and I soon found myself on my way back home.

My father was by himself, because David was a tank commander in Italy. I found myself full of jealousy because I had had to get out of the service, while my kid brother was right in the thick of things. Now here I was at home, expected to climb back in the nest and get down to business as usual.

I moved in with my father and started working for my brother Eddie. It wasn't the best of arrangements, but I knew it was expected of me.

After a time, I started back to the yeshiva to complete my rabbinical training. My father had had his heart set on this for so many years, that it just had to become a reality. He couldn't remember a generation that didn't have an Esses as a rabbi, and I was the only hope for this generation.

When David was discharged from the Army, he came back to live with my dad and me. David came to work with Eddie also, so we were together all of the time, except when I was at the yeshiva. We used to double-date, and this was the place where a little jealousy crept in — my jealousy, not David's. He was such a good-looking guy that he was awfully tough competition. When he walked down the street, the girls would stand stock-still, and just stare at him. The only redeeming aspect of this situation was that David seemed totally unaware of how good-looking he was.

Finally, the long-awaited day of my ordination came, and I had the satisfaction of knowing that I had made my father happy. The line had not been broken.

Now came a time for a major decision. Where would I minister for the Lord? The logical place was with my father right there in Brooklyn. Dad and I both prayed fervently for direction. One evening my dad told me something so bizarre that I knew it could not have come from my father. He said, "The burden of the Lord has come upon me to direct you to go to California."

I was completely dumbfounded. I asked my father, "What kind of a Lord are we serving? It would be tough enough getting started here, much less in California." My dad maintained that I should be obedient, and I knew this direction must be from God, as my father knew nothing about California. Since coming to America, he had not been out of Brooklyn.

I procrastinated taking any action for as long as I could, but finally the day came when I reluctantly boarded a train for Los Angeles. I hated to leave the only home I had ever known, the people I had grown up with, and most of all David.

David had promised that he would join me as soon as Eddie could get someone to replace him in the store. He told me, "Don't worry, buddy, you won't be alone out there with all those movie actresses long. I won't be far behind you."

When I arrived in Los Angeles, I must say I liked what I saw. I was so used to the dreary, dark buildings of New York, and its extreme weather conditions, that all these pastel colors drenched in sunshine made quite an impression on me. The people also appeared different. The ever-present sunshine seemed to brighten their spirits also; they seemed much friendlier than the average bellicose New Yorker.

Some childhood friends of mine had a store in Santa Monica, a suburb of Los Angeles, so I looked them up. I was welcomed with open arms, so I found myself staying in this lovely beach city. I settled down and proceeded to wait for what the Lord had in store for me. Little did I know what a hard test I would be put through and how badly I would fail it.

I received a call from David on March 31, 1950, saying, "Prepare the way for me." He was driving out to join me in Santa Monica. On April second I received a second call, this one from the Texas Highway Patrol.

My first thoughts were, "They've got my crazy brother in jail—he was probably speeding, and now I'm going to have to bail him out."

A deep voice came over the phone, saying, "Is this Michael Esses, the brother of David Esses?" I said, "Yes, what's the trouble?"

My brother David had been killed at approximately six in the morning. His convertible had rammed into a huge trailer truck. Two thirds of the car had gone underneath the truck. David had been decapitated. The patrolman said he was sorry that he had to give me such news, and that I should call them if they could do anything for me. Then he hung up.

"Do anything for me? Why don't you just shoot me and get it over with?" My mind cried out the words, but no audible words could come. I was trying to shut off my mind completely. This was something I couldn't accept, I couldn't believe, I couldn't assimilate. In fact, I wouldn't even try. The phone hadn't rung, it was all a bad dream, and I would wake up at any moment.

After a length of time, reality started to sink in, and I fell into a million pieces. I cried out the age-old question, why? over and over again, but all I received as an answer was an echo of my own words. I felt as though my heart had surely broken and that if you cut me open, you could put your hand into my stomach and pick up the ball of grief that was there.

Then the hate that had been silently living inside of me since my mother's death blossomed in full bloom. A lie, it's always been one big lie. There's no God, there couldn't be. If there was a God, things like this wouldn't happen. I knew then that my whole life had been a farce.

This was my frame of mind when I called my father to tell him that his youngest son was dead. I very bluntly told him that his precious God had allowed David to die a horrible death and that I wanted no part of his God anymore.

I guess I expected to hear an audible gasp on the other end of the line when I hurled these words from 3,000 miles away. What I heard was complete silence for a few minutes; then a quiet voice said, "What happened, son? Tell me the details."

My dad's calmness infuriated me. I gave him the gory details of David's death with absolutely no thought about making it easier for him. When I had finished, I waited for the cry that I knew must be welling up in him. What I heard next was more than I could fathom. Softly came the words,

> Praise the name of the Lord,
> Blessed be the name of the Lord from this day
>   forth and forever more.
> The Lord giveth and the Lord taketh away
> Blessed be the name of the Lord. Amen.

At this point, I lost the little composure I had left, and I started to rail against God. I asked my dad where was the God that we had served? I told him that if this was his idea of a just and faithful God, I wanted no part of Him. I said that I hated and despised Him, and that if my dad was smart, he would feel the same way. By this time I was yelling that the Lord his God had repaid him for his faithfulness all these years by taking his wife and now his son away from him.

My dad quietly answered this tirade by saying that he knew how upset I was and that in time I would see that I would have to ask the Lord's forgiveness. My father's choice of words could not have been worse, as far as I was concerned. I dogmatically said, "I will never as long as I live ever speak to God again, much less ask His forgiveness, and that is final."

My father ended the conversation by saying that he would send my brother Eddie to Texas to bring back David's body. He wanted to know how long it would take me to get home for the funeral. I told him that I refused to go home to the funeral where I would have to hear praise after praise to a Deity that didn't even exist. My father hung up with the words, "May God have mercy on you, my son."

The bitterness in me was complete, as complete as my rejection of God. I felt He had basely betrayed me, first with my mother and now with David. I found it impossible to love Him or praise Him. All I could do was hate Him and everyone who represented Him. I had gone from being a rabbi to a despiser of God in one lesson.

The basic difference between my father and me when we encountered David's death was that my belief in God was shallow and my father's was like a rock. My faith was something that had been forced on me from the age of two, and I had never had a personal relationship with God. I was a rabbi who had no love for the Lord.

My father's relationship with God was a different matter. He was intimate with God—Jehovah, the God of Abraham, Isaac, and Jacob. They were friends, and no sacrifice unto God was too much to ask of him. This was why he could praise God at the time of his son's death, because he believed God. The moment he heard of David's death, he knew without a doubt that his son was in the presence of the Lord.

As far as I was concerned, David would be six feet under, and God would be far away, a fairy tale you read to gullible children out of a book.

11

"THE LORD had a plan." "The Lord had a plan." "The Lord had a plan." This phrase accompanies the drone of the motors as we wing across the Atlantic toward England. I glance around and see that most of our group has settled down for the night. A survey out the window tells me that we're hurtling toward the black abyss of night ahead of us. No more pinpoints of lights below to assure you of civilization. Just darkness, which I begin to equate with the darkness of my soul after David's death. No man is so lost as the man who has left God.

I glance over at my wife. She is curled up in her seat, already fast asleep. I love her for being patient with me today, listening to me reminisce about the years before she knew me. All of these years are hard to remember, but the months after David's death were probably the worst.

As I look back on those months, I don't remember consciously deciding to go Satan's way. I realize that I had turned my back on God, so I should have known that the results were inevitable. This is where the phrase, "The Lord had a plan," comes in, because maybe I had turned my back on Him but He hadn't turned His back on me. When I look down at the girl sleeping quietly beside me, I know without a doubt that the long arm of God reached out and found the one person in this world who would be able to see me through the miserable years ahead.

Since I was a Jew from such a strict Jewish family, I never considered that I would ever become seriously involved with any girl who wasn't Jewish and preferably a Sephardic Jew. There had been lots of casual girlfriends in my life, and I guess I considered myself quite a man-about-town, one who really played the field. I hadn't reckoned with a cute brown-eyed Irish girl who wouldn't take no for an answer.

I was working in a gift shop in downtown Santa Monica. Next-door was a J. J. Newberry's. They had a snack bar, and lots of teenage waitresses working there. I used to go in every morning and have a typical Jewish breakfast of chocolate pie and a chocolate milkshake.

As any man will do, I looked the girls over. Even though they weren't bad-looking—in fact a couple of them were dolls—I dismissed them as being much too young for me. I was an older, sophisticated man of twenty-six at this time. Yet I found myself drawn to one particular little waitress. She was seventeen, small, very pretty, with big beautiful eyes, long dark hair, and quite a personality. It wasn't hard to tell that she was a favorite with the other girls and the customers, too. Her name was Betty, and she was as Irish as they come.

Every day you could find me eating my unorthodox breakfast in Betty's section of the fountain, but never seriously considering asking her out. Where would you take a kid like that anyway? Skating, to a hamburger stand, maybe to a kiddie movie?

I didn't know at the time that Betty was also well aware of me and wondering when I would approach her for a date. With the typical lack of finesse of a teenager, she concocted a plan to really get my attention. For well over two weeks, she saved a bottle of sour milk, letting it get a little more sour every day. Finally came the day that she deemed it just right.

Now enters Beau Brummel, the sophisticated man-about-town, the man who could handle himself in any situation, certainly anything this little girl could come up with. I sat down at Betty's section of the counter and ordered my breakfast. In no time, a beautiful thick milkshake was sitting in front of me.

I lifted the brimming icy glass to my lips and took a big swallow. I couldn't believe my taste buds — the top of my head was coming off! I had never tasted anything so atrocious in my life. I gave a quick look at Betty, and she was standing there with her eyes looking toward heaven, an angelic expression upon her face. I knew then that she had mixed this concoction on purpose.

Many thoughts went through my mind; murder was probably the nicest one. But one thing was sure — I wasn't going to give her the satisfaction of hearing me yell about the shake. So with all the aplomb of a man drinking the nectar of the gods, I downed the rest of the shake, smiled my thanks, paid my bill, walked nonchalantly out the door, went into the gift shop next-door, and threw up.

I'll have to admit one thing about the milkshake episode. Betty did get my attention. In fact, what was shortly going to be my undivided attention. The next day I bought tickets to the wrestling matches and asked Betty to go with me. I figured this was something a kid would probably enjoy, and at this time, in 1951, wrestling was the big rage on TV and everybody was watching it.

Betty said she'd be glad to go with me, that she had never been to see a match before. So promptly at seven o'clock, I arrived at her home to pick her up. Betty's mother opened the door and invited me in, and I spent the next half hour making small talk with her father and mother. I could tell they weren't too thrilled with me, and wondered why their daughter had agreed to go out with a man as old as I was. Obviously, I wasn't an Irishman. I did not know it at the time, but Betty's sister, Joan, was also going with a Jewish boy.

Betty finally made her appearance, and I must say she was worth waiting for. I had seen her only in her uniform, and now she had on a blue suit and was wearing high heels. She looked every inch a woman, and I was proud to have her on my arm.

I was beginning to wonder if I had made a mistake about where I was taking her on our first date. I had never been to one of these matches either, and of course everybody knew they were phony. When we arrived at the Olympic Auditorium, I had never seen such a mixture of people in my life. Their attire ranged from blue jeans to evening dresses, and included everything in-between.

I had purchased ringside seats, so we were close enough to really see the shenanigans. The only way I can sum up that evening is to say that I have never laughed harder or had more fun in my life. Betty took it all so seriously. When she saw the golden curls on him and saw how unfair one wrestler named Gorgeous George was, she got furious. Everyone sitting around us was having as good a time watching her as they were watching the match.

When we got back to her home, Betty invited me in. She said she'd fix us a snack, and we could talk for a little while in the kitchen. Her mom and dad were asleep, so we had the house to ourselves. She opened a can of chili, and we sat down and started talking about the crazy match we had seen. To this day, I can't remember what I said, but it must have been funny, and Betty had just taken a bite of chili. You guessed it. All over my suit.

Anyone who knows me knows that no one could be

more fastidious than I am. If anything could be calculated to turn me off, this would be it. But I found myself laughing even harder than she was. This little girl already had me hooked, and I didn't have the slightest idea how it had happened.

After this inauspicious beginning, Betty and I were together constantly. I would come by each morning and pick her up and take her to work, bring her back home, and take her out nearly every evening. My biggest problem was all her old boyfriends from Santa Monica High. To me they were all just young squirts, but I still didn't want them around.

One evening Betty, her father and mother, sister Joan and her boyfriend, and I went to a dance. We were seated in the enclosure where they served drinks, and there was an armed guard at the entrance. There were a couple of old friends of Betty's there. I fended them off most of the evening by not leaving her side for a second. There was only one problem. I had to go to the men's room, in the worst way. I knew if I left Betty, these two guys who were circling like vultures would close in. I stalled as long as possible, but after an hour, it was very apparent to me that I had to put this Jewish mind to work and solve my problem in a hurry. Then I got an idea. I left the table and went over and told the armed guard about my situation. He was a very understanding man, and with much flourishing and brandishing of weapons, he came over and stood guard over my girl until I returned from the men's room. My father was right. He always told me, "When you need help, ask a policeman."

Betty and I continued to keep company for the next few months, and it became obvious that marriage was on the horizon. I knew what my family's reaction would be. The only way I could handle the situation as far as they were concerned was to make it an accomplished fact. I was 3,000 miles away from home, and they had no idea that I was even going with a Gentile.

Betty's mother and dad were a different story. We had gotten to be good friends, but they could see too many pitfalls for the two of us, not to have lots of reservations when it came to marriage. Our backgrounds couldn't have been more opposite. I was Jew, and Betty was an Irish Presbyterian. Religion had never been the big thing in her family that it was in mine, but when you start talking about intermarriage, religion takes on giant proportions.

I was a big-city boy who was a son of immigrants. She was a small-town girl, daughter of people whose family practically came over on the Mayflower. I had had an unhappy childhood of total restriction. She had had a wonderful childhood with a freedom I couldn't even imagine.

Betty had spent her childhood years in Hobbs, New Mexico, where her father was superintendent of the Landreth Oil Company. As a child, Betty had lived out on an oil lease — a few company homes out on miles and miles of prairie. She and her sister Joan had roamed all over that country on their horses, herding sheep, chasing a stray cow, inspecting the prairie-dog homes, swimming in an "old swimming hole," doing all the things a child can do when raised in the wide-open spaces. In the evening, Betty's dad would climb up on an oil derrick and look out over the prairie for his girls. When he had them spotted, he would take off in a pickup truck and herd them back home.

Later, Betty's family moved to Sweetwater, Texas where, as Betty puts it, "We were big frogs in an awfully small pond."

Her family belonged to the country club, and Betty and Joan used to sit wide-eyed, watching their mother and dad dress in evening clothes for dances and many other social events. Her father was president of the Jaycees and the

Lions Club. He played tournament golf in New Mexico and Texas, with his family often accompanying him. Betty's mother played bridge with the mayor's wife and had a colored girl at home to help with the house and her girls. The girls' birthday parties were reported on the social page of the local newspaper.

Until she met me, Betty had never even known a Jewish person. There were no Jews in her hometown, so fortunately for us, she had absolutely no feelings of prejudice at all. As she says, "The subject never came up. It would have been like talking about someone from another world."

As you've probably ascertained, I decided to make Betty my wife anyway. I knew there would be lots of problems, but I couldn't imagine living the rest of my life without her. The first matter that I had to deal with myself about was that Betty had no idea that I was a rabbi who had turned his back on God. Betty was a "Christian" in the sense that she had been raised in the framework of the Protestant church. I knew her faith was not a major part of her life as mine had been, yet I knew that she would have been appalled that I had turned completely away from God, so I decided to keep quiet on this subject.

One night, after a beautiful meal at a restaurant overlooking the ocean, we walked out on the balcony to watch the surf break on the rocks below. I told Betty that I wanted to set a date, and that I wanted to tell her folks that we were going to be married. She said that she wanted to be married by a minister, that she wouldn't feel married unless a man of God performed the ceremony.

I don't know why this came as a complete surprise to me, but it did. I had decided on a quick trip to Las Vegas and a visit to a Justice of the Peace, but Betty said that either a minister married us or there would be no marriage. It made me mad for her to be so adamant. In a fit of temper, I told her that there was no way she was going to get me in a church, so she could just forget the whole thing. That was just too much of an ultimatum for Betty's Irish temper, so instead of it being the wonderful night that I envisioned, it ended up a nightmare. By the time I got her home, two wills were in total combat.

I had played right into the hands of Betty's folks. Even though they liked me personally, they could seen no hopes for a successful union. So when Betty came home in tears, crying that we had broken up for good, her dad and mother were ready with a plan.

Betty's dad was retired, so he wasn't held by anything in Santa Monica. Her sister Joan's boyfriend was in the service overseas, so there was no reason for her to have to stay in Santa Monica. Betty's dad and mother proposed moving up to Portland, Oregon, so that Betty would have a better chance to get over this infatuation.

Not knowing all this, about two weeks later, I thought I would look Betty up. I figured she had probably cooled down by now, and would be prepared to listen to reason. I had no intention of letting her go, and I felt this separation would have let her know who was boss.

I walked into Newberry's for breakfast and was greeted by the girls with, "Hi, Mike, where have you been?" "Glad to see you," etc. I looked around, but I didn't see Betty. I could feel the tension in the air, and I wondered what was up. All the girls knew Betty and I had been going together for months. Finally I asked, "Where's my girl?" There was a very pregnant pause before one of the girls said, "She's moved to Oregon, Mike." I must have done a classic double take. "She's what?" Then they told me about her going with her folks to Oregon.

I walked out of the store in a state of shock. "How could she do this to me?" Well, believe me, this wasn't going to be the end of this story, not as long as I was alive and breathing. In fact, nothing could have been calculated to make me more determined that Betty was going to be my wife.

I went to see her grandmother, who lived at the beach in Santa Monica. I begged her to give me Betty's address in Portland, and after much persuasion, she relented and gave it to me. She and I had always been the best of friends. She was a deeply religious woman, and she always said that if she hadn't been raised a Christian she would have wanted to be a Jew, because that was what her Jesus was.

I went to see my boss and told him I had some business I had to attend to, and that I needed a few days off. He agreed to give me the time I needed. He was well aware something was brewing, because of the caliber of work I had managed to do—or rather not to do—the last couple of weeks.

Now began two days of driving and scheming and telling myself I was a fool. There was a running battle going on in my mind. One side said, "Keep going. You don't want to lose her," while the other side told me what an idiot I was to even bother with a girl who would pull a trick like this.

I arrived at Portland in the midst of a downpour, and I began to search for the address I had been given by Betty's grandmother. After a million wrong streets, I found the house. It was perched on the side of a hill in one of the suburbs of Portland. I was ill-equipped to be out in the rain —after all, two days ago I was in sunny California—so by the time I got to the front door I was thoroughly soaked.

As I raised my hand to knock, I was assailed with fear. Many thoughts crowded their way into my mind, thoughts like, "Is this really what you want?" "Why don't you let well enough alone?" "What are you going to do if the door is slammed in your face?" "No woman is worth all this aggravation." Yet I found myself rapping on the door and waiting with a pounding heart for the door to open.

It was Betty who opened it. She just stood and stared

at me for a moment. Then she threw herself in my arms crying like a baby. I found myself crying, too, and saying I didn't care who married us, just as long as we were married.

Betty's mother and father had gone to Eugene for a couple of days, and they weren't expected back until that night, so we decided that we would elope. She packed a bag and left her folks a note telling them that I had come to get her, and that we were going away to get married.

As we were so close to the Canadian border, we headed for Victoria, British Columbia. This is where we were married and spent our honeymoon. Oh, by the way, we were married at Saint Andrews Presbyterian Church.

After a few days, we headed back to Portland with much apprehension. Betty had no idea how her dad and mother were going to take our marriage now that it was an accomplished fact. We needn't have worried, because they welcomed us both with open arms. They are two of the kindest people you would ever want to meet, and now that their daughter was married, they wouldn't do anything to cause that marriage trouble. I know now that they figured there was going to be enough trouble without any help from them.

Betty and I talked it over and decided we would stay in Portland for a while. I went out and made the rounds, looking for a job, and after a few days, I was employed at Eastern Department Store as a children's-wear buyer. I had no previous experience in this line, but it didn't take me long to know what I was doing.

It would be nice to be able to say that Betty and I were as happy as all newlyweds should be, but when you're dealing with someone as warped as I was, you have a hard time keeping things smooth.

Betty was a normal wife, in love with her husband, but she was not prepared to lie down and become a doormat. This is what I demanded of her. I would not brook any disagreements, and when an argument loomed on the horizon, I would just about go berserk. I could see absolutely no reason for any kind of an argument. I could not remember one argument between my father and mother, and I wanted to have the same kind of relationship. I felt that as long as I was supporting her, she should be happy to do anything I wanted her to do.

Betty was totally unable to handle someone like me. In the first place, she was too young; and in the second place, she had never been around someone who acted like I did. Do you remember the finger in the light switch when I was a kid? I never outgrew this behavior. When Betty would give me a bad time about anything, no matter how small and insignificant, I would sit bare-chested in front of an open window, letting the cold wind and snow hit my body. I would hope I would get pneumonia. Then I figured she would be sorry she had crossed me. I used this kind of retribution against her for things like telling me to go get my own glass of water.

Betty says you've never lived until you've been burned at the stake for not getting someone a glass of water. She had come from a home where her father thought nothing of helping with the dishes, helping to clean house, or going to get a glass of water himself.

This is what Betty's parents had been afraid of when they contemplated our marriage between such diverse backgrounds. They knew Betty had been brought up in the modern American way, where a man and woman were helpmates instead of one being in command and the other being subordinate. They knew that I, in turn, had been raised where a woman cares for her husband's needs, whatever they happen to be, and is happy to do whatever is required to make him happy.

One of the things that never ceased to grate on me was Betty's need to go to church. She was always asking me to take her, and when I told her to count me out, that she could go by herself, she would refuse, saying, "We should be together like a family." She finally wore me down after a time by an extremely clever maneuver. She would strike at night after we had gone to bed. That was when the nudge would come in my side and the water-torture drip of, "Honey, when are you going to take me to church?" would begin. I finally agreed to go, and one Sunday found me in a position even I couldn't believe.

I was walking down the aisle, complete with a red rose in my lapel, ready to join the church and be baptized. The whole scene was blowing my mind, but I didn't know how to get out of it. In fact, I didn't even know how I got into it. Betty was at my side, looking like the cat that had swallowed the canary. To made a long story short, I emerged thirty minutes later a bonafide "Christian."

One thing I have to say about that church—they were really on the ball. The very next day there was a letter in the mail from the stewardship committee asking for my pledge. All of the resentment I had felt for being put in such a ridiculous position in the first place exploded. Without a moment's hesitation, I reached for a red pencil, and wrote across the letter, "Me? Give *you* *my* money? DROP DEAD." Then, with dispatch, I mailed it back special delivery.

Unfortunately for them, two members of other committees made the mistake of calling me on the next two days. One was from the Mariners, a social and service organization in the Presbyterian church. I also received a call from the Christian education committee. They knew of my extensive knowledge of the Old Testament, and they wanted me to teach an adult class. I am ashamed to say that both of these men heard a reply that more or less coincided with the red-pencil scrawl on the stewardship letter. I had made one more giant step in my life. I was now even a worse Christian than I was a Jew.

Since things were not going my way at home, it wasn't long before I was involved in my first affair. The woman worked in the same store as I did, and after going to lunch together a few times, we had come to a mutual understanding: I wouldn't do anything to jeopardize her marriage, and she wouldn't do anything to jeopardize mine.

I had walked away from God, but He was still with me, working out His plan. I was fourteen years old when I had rheumatic fever the first time, and now, after all those years, I had a recurrence. The doctor advised me to get out of the damp cold weather of Portland.

Betty and I decided to go to Florida for a few months until the sun could bake me back to good health. We figured that by that time we would know what to do about our future. Betty bundled me into the car midst pillows and blankets and started the long drive across country.

I remember lying there watching her drive, with all the sin I had committed against her marching in review in front of my eyes. I was thankful that she didn't know the extent to which I had gone, and I was grateful that she was with me in spite of the treatment she had received.

We stayed in Florida for only about six months; then we were off to Philadelphia, Pennsylvania, where I worked in another gift store for my livelihood. Things were going steadily from bad to worse for Betty and me, and in a short time, I was on the lookout again for someone to feed my ego, someone who didn't know what I was really like, someone who lacked enough in character herself to make me look and feel good. I was staying away from home more and more.

12

ONE DAY while I was at work, Betty called me on the phone, and told me that my family was trying to get in touch with me. Since my marriage, the relationship with all my relatives had been very strained, to put it mildly, so I knew it must be an emergency for them to attempt to contact me.

I knew before I made the call that it would be about my father. I had seen him a couple of months earlier, and he had been in very bad condition at that time. He was being cared for in a nursing home in New York. It tore me up so much when I saw him that my usual behavior pattern when faced with something unpleasant went into effect.

I closed my eyes and my mind and escaped from the fact that my father was dying. I knew, underneath it all, that the last person who cared enough for me to present me to the Lord was about to leave this world, and I didn't want to acknowledge it.

I made the phone call to New York with a fearful heart, and it was as I suspected. My father had passed away over the Memorial Day weekend.

Now my turmoil was complete. Betty and I were practically separated, and my father was dead. I was in a state of total depression when I attended my dad's funeral. This same feeling was with me when I returned to the mess I was making out of my life in Philadelphia. As usual, I was busy pushing my own private destruct button as I attempted to wreck my relationship with the only person left who cared about me.

This was when Betty and I had a showdown. I told her that I didn't want her anymore, and I didn't care what she did. Whereas she had always been hysterical when I talked like this to her before, this time she was calm. In fact, she seemed downright serene about the whole thing. Right in front of me, she picked up the phone, placed a long-distance call to her folks in Santa Monica, and told them that we were through. She asked if they would come to Philadelphia and help her dispose of some of her furniture and then aid her in getting the rest of it back to California.

Her dad told her they would get there as soon as they could. In the meantime, she could put an ad in the paper and sell all the big pieces of furniture.

By this time it was beginning to sink in that she was going to take me up on my proposition. In a fog, I heard her tell her parents that she loved them. Then she hung up the phone. She promptly picked it up again and dialed the local paper and placed an ad putting our furniture up for sale. Even though I had told her this was what I wanted, it made me furious for her to so calmly start selling off our life together piece by piece. I stomped out of the apartment, vowing never to see her again.

I can't tell you what I did the next couple of days. The world had been pulled out from under me. Betty was the only other person except for my mother who had ever represented security to me, and here I was, throwing it away. I found myself lamenting, "Why does someone destroy what he loves? Why does someone toss out the only decent thing in his life like so much garbage?" Finally I decided even I couldn't be this much of a fool, and I went home to ask Betty to stay with me.

When I arrived at the apartment, I was in for a big surprise. Practically all of the furniture was already sold. The place was nearly empty, and there were half-packed cartons all over the place. My appearance had taken Betty unawares, and I could tell she didn't know how to act with me.

For the first time in all our years of marriage, I asked her to forgive me. I told her that life would be totally empty without her, and I begged her not to leave me. With a great deal of love, she told me that this had been all my idea, not hers, and that she would always love me. But she said she knew she would be unable to stay in Philadelphia, because of all the hurt she had sustained here. My heart dropped with such a thud that I barely heard her next words. She added that if I wanted to come back with her to Santa Monica, it was fine with her. I asked her to repeat what she had just said, and when she did, I threw my arms around her and cried like a baby.

I felt bad about Betty's folks making the big trip to get her, but there were no words of reproach from them, just love. I can remember thinking how lucky I was to have become involved with a family who loved each other so much that there was even enough love left over to cover a fool like me.

Within a week's time, we were back in Santa Monica where the whole odyssey had begun years before. It was 1955, and I was looking for a job.

My sister-in-law's husband, Gene, was in the parking-lot business, and he took me in and trained me. It wasn't long before I knew what I was doing well enough to have obtained a few lots of my own.

The parking-lot business is a peculiar business; you can

make good money for your investment. There is only one thing it requires of you. Time, unlimited time. I used to go to work at ten in the morning and work till three the next morning. The only way I ever got to see my wife was when she came down to sit in the lots to keep me company.

You make your money in a lot from the tips the customers give the boys who park their cars. As owner of the lot, I had the tips turned over to me, and I paid the boys a salary. I wasn't going to take the chance of losing any of those tips, so I was always on the job.

During this time, I received through the mail a New Testament written in Hebrew. There was a return address of a publishing house in England, but not a clue of who had sent it to me. I still don't know who sent it. One day, out of curiosity, and because it was written in Hebrew, I took it to work with me and proceeded to read it. I identified with this man Jesus, because He was raised as I was raised. I was glad I read the book, because even though I didn't think Jesus was the Messiah, I no longer felt the animosity I had always felt toward Him. I showed my regard for Him by taking the book home, sticking it on the top shelf of the bookcase, and promptly forgetting about it.

Life was fairly tranquil for the next few years, except when Betty and I would go round and round periodically over my gambling. This was my new vice, and I was really more involved than she knew. The main reason I was so involved was because I had Satan on my side. It was phenomenal how often I would win. It didn't matter whether I was betting on the horses, a football game, baseball, or whatever, I won about 90 percent of the time. I began to spend all my idle hours at the parking lots, figuring out the horses.

In 1959, we moved to Anaheim, California, a town approximately twenty-five miles from Los Angeles. The acquisition of a custom drapery business precipitated our move. Betty and I were having more and more trouble, mainly because I was never at home, and it was a very lonely life for her. When I was at home, I was usually giving her a bad time, because I was always busy making mountains out of every molehill that came along. As usual, when things got too bad, I always wanted to make a move. What I never understood was that I kept taking the worst troublemaker along with me — myself.

Nineteen fifty-nine was a banner year for Betty and me because of the move to Anaheim and another extraordinary event. In October we learned that Betty was pregnant. Over the years, we had wanted children, but Betty had been told that she would never become pregnant, so we had forgotten about a family.

Now after all these years, a baby was on its way. We were both thrilled, except for one cloud on the horizon. The doctor took X rays and told us the prognosis was a difficult birth. The doctor wanted Betty to have a natural delivery, if possible, because the odds would be in favor of the baby. He felt that Betty's pregnancy was a fluke, that she probably would never be pregnant again, so he didn't want to take any chances with the child.

Betty went into labor on April first in the afternoon. She was very calm when she called me home from the store, but I can't say as much for myself. I had been driving her nuts for the past couple of months. Every time she would go to sleep at night, she would wake up with a start, because I would be feeling her stomach. I was scared to death that she would go into labor and not know it. Then I would have to deliver the baby at home.

It was a little hard to explain to the policeman who was behind me when I skidded into my driveway that this was an emergency, because Betty was in the house taking a shower. I started shouting at her something to the effect of *"Of all times to be clean!"* She told the officer about my condition, and he just grinned and offered to escort us to the hospital. Betty thanked him, but said we'd be all right, that she still had to pack her bag. I could have killed her. Mentally, I started taking inventory: boiling water, clean sheets, scissors, a string to tie the cord, etc. It was at about this point that Betty came out dressed and ready to go.

The next few hours were a total nightmare for me. I vowed that I'd never go through this again. I didn't leave Betty's side for a moment in the labor room although she kept begging me to. She kept mumbling something about me making her nervous. *Her nervous!* I was way past that stage. When they started wheeling her into the delivery room, it was 2:00 in the morning. At the door of the delivery room they told me to kiss my wife good-bye, that I'd see her in a little while. I told them no way, that I was going with her. The nurse was very firm and held me back while they pushed Betty ahead into the room. My little daughter came into this world while her father stood outside banging on the doors of the delivery room yelling, "Let me IN."

"Sugar and spice and everything nice." Nothing had prepared me for the love I felt for this little girl. At last there seemed to be some meaning for my existence. For the first time in many years, I felt my heart open enough to feel real tenderness. I couldn't wait to get home every night so I could give Kathleen her bottle before she went to bed.

When Kathy was about two months old, she developed colic, and night after night I walked the floor with her. It wasn't a chore. It was a privilege I cherished. When she would finally fall asleep in my arms, I couldn't bear to put her down. I used to sit in the rocking chair, and look into that tiny face, with its button nose, and dream of the years ahead. I saw her as a little girl full of hugs and kisses and ruffled petticoats, as a girl gangly as a young colt, as a teenager talking her old dad out of a new cashmere sweater, even as a bride on her father's arm, looking radiant and beautiful. Sometimes the love I felt for her would overwhelm me, and we would just sit quietly, my daughter and I, while tears of joy rolled down my face.

I needed Betty's help in the store, so we bought an extra crib and took Kathy right along with us. She was the darling of the business people downtown. They had watched Betty carry her for all those months, and they all felt like godparents to her.

When Kathy was three months old, Betty took her to the pediatrician for her monthly well-baby check and her first DPT shot. When Betty got back to the store, she laid Kathy in her crib, and in a few minutes she was involved with a customer. I was on the phone when I heard an odd sound, and I looked over into the crib. What I saw nearly frightened me to death. The baby's eyes were turned up into her head, and her whole body was jerking spasmodically. I yelled at Betty, and we grabbed the baby and ran. The doctor's office was fifteen minutes from the store, but I made it in five. We ran into the office with Kathleen still in this terrible condition. The nurse took her from us and told us to sit down before we both collapsed. In a few minutes, the doctor came out and told us she was having a convulsion. They didn't know what had caused it, so they wanted to put her in the hospital to make some tests.

Reluctantly, we agreed, and Kathy was taken from us and put in the contagious-disease ward at Orange County Hospital. The next two days were a nightmare, because we couldn't be with her, and we knew she must feel so frightened and alone. We also knew some of the tests, like the spinal tap, were quite painful. Finally, after all the tests were evaluated, we were told that Kathy had had an anaphylactoid (hypersensitive) reaction to quadrigen, the drug that had been given to her in her DPT shot. We were reassured that she would probably be all right now, but that we should watch her closely.

I knew that Betty had been in constant prayer, and I must admit that I had sent up a few pleas myself, just in case He *was* there.

The next few months were happy ones, because Kathy seemed fine, and another miracle was on its way. Yes, another baby was due in March, just eleven months after Kathy's birthday.

Early in December, I received a call from home telling me to get there as fast as possible. It was one of my neighbors calling, and I could hear Betty crying in the background. I got home as fast as I could, and as I drove up, I could see the red fire-rescue truck in front of our house. I ran in to find two firemen leaning over my baby. She had an oxygen mask over her face.

Betty was hysterical, so I couldn't get anything out of her, but our neighbor Lenore told me that Kathy had gone into a convulsion again, and that Betty had called the fire department. After about thirty minutes, the firemen said that Kathy seemed all right enough to be taken to our doctor. He set up an appointment at Children's Hospital in Los Angeles for a complete neurological checkup.

After a week of extensive testing, we were given the verdict. The doctor at Children's sat us down in his office and told us that Kathy was brain-damaged, that she was epileptic, and that there would be retardation. Time would tell to what degree.

How do you take news like this? You walk out of the hospital holding your baby tightly to you, wanting desperately to shield her from all that's ahead, and you really don't know how you can bear to live another moment except you have to. What would *she* do without you? There were no words said on the long drive back to Anaheim. I couldn't bear to look at Betty. The bewilderment and agony mirrored in her eyes made me think of a wounded animal.

When we arrived back home, Betty tenderly bathed a tired little baby, fed her, and put her to bed, where she fell into a deep peaceful sleep, unaware of her parents who were lying in each other's arms, sobbing over a little girl with no future.

The next couple of months were very hard on Betty and me. We could see that Kathy was losing ground both mentally and physically. In February, we had our worst night. Kathy had gone into status epilepsy—when there is one convulsive seizure after another. We had been in constant contact with our doctor, and he finally said, "Bring her into the hospital. I'll be waiting for you."

It was nearly midnight, and I was driving as fast as I could. Betty was holding Kathy in her arms, bent over her, listening for her breathing. My mind was whirling, trying to figure the fastest route to the hospital, when out of silence in the car I heard Betty say, "Mike, she's dead. Our baby's dead." My foot floorboarded the accelerator as my mind refused to accept the words that Betty was saying over and over: "She's dead, she's dead, she's dead."

When we arrived at the emergency room, I jumped out and tried to take the baby from Betty, but she wouldn't let go of her. She just clutched her to her breast and walked into the hospital like a zombie, in a total state of shock. All she would say was, "My baby's dead," again and again. When she saw our doctor, she went to him and laid the baby in his arms, and with a cry that soon became a wail, she cried, "My baby's dead."

The doctor laid Kathy on the examining table and put the stethoscope to her chest. In a moment, he raised his head and said, "She's alive. She's just in a comatose state, recovering from all the seizures she's had." He explained that she was breathing within, not outwardly, so that Betty could not hear or feel her breathing. The doctor then put

Betty and Kathy to bed in the same hospital room so they could recover from this ordeal.

Out of this horrible experience, Betty and I realized we had to know what we were dealing with, so we read everything we could get our hands on about epilepsy.

March 6, 1961, our son, John Michael, was born. Betty had no trouble having him, but I must confess I made a fool of myself at the hospital again. I overheard the nurse talking to Betty's obstetrician. She said, "I've seen nervous fathers before, but this one is ridiculous." I tried to get hold of myself, but whenever Betty is in any kind of physical danger, I *panic*. Everyone who had ever meant anything to me had been taken from me suddenly without any warning, and I lived in fear that it would happen again.

The next couple of years I was the victim of a variety of emotions. There were times when my family was everything to me, but the selfish man was still there. The two babies took most of Betty's time, patience, and interest — especially Kathy. Betty's constant care, trying one method after another of getting food into her, made the difference between life and death to the child. About the only time she could get her to eat was while she was asleep. Every night I would find Betty leaning over the crib, giving Kathy a bottle while she was sound asleep. It would take hours, but Betty wouldn't give up. She was eventually rewarded, when Kathy started to rally and get stronger physically day by day.

I wouldn't have had Betty do differently, but I was surely feeling the pangs of a neglected husband. And then we received some astounding news. Betty was pregnant again! This meant three babies in diapers, besides all the other work around the house. We were both happy about the baby, but we dreaded telling people that another child was on the way. We knew most of our friends would think we were crazy.

Laurie Michele was born on January 17, 1963.

I love my children very much and have been accused of being a typical Jewish mother. There is nothing I wouldn't do for any of our children. All of our babies developed colic, and I can't begin to count the nights that I walked the floor with them, or took them in their infant seats for a ride in the car to soothe them until they fell asleep. I loved their mother also, but in the midst of our relationship, there continued to be a self-destruct button in me that I couldn't help pressing.

Betty was making me nervous again with her talk about God being the only answer for peace of mind over Kathy. It seemed like she was totally perverse with her timing. Every time Kathy had a seizure, I would just about put my fist through the wall. I couldn't stand it, and the rage that would sweep over me had to be directed somewhere. The more Betty talked about the Lord, the madder I got. We would end up screaming at each other, two adults, each hurting in his own particular way, over the crib of a baby in the throes of a convulsion. It was a scene straight out of hell each time it happened.

Pretty soon I felt that desperate need to escape again, into whatever misadventure it would take to make me forget the pain at home. As usual, when I was ready to take such a step, Satan was right there with the opportunity. It wasn't long before I was involved again with someone who was willing to give my ego the boost it needed. Only this time, Betty found out about it.

I have heard all my life that hell hath no fury like a woman scorned. I would have much preferred hell in comparison to what I heard from Betty when she found out that I was unfaithful. She ranted, she raved, she called me every name in the book, and I know that if she had had a gun in her hand, she would have shot me. Yet I would have preferred this to what happened after the first shock was over. When the fury left, the hurt set in.

After Betty had put the children to bed that night, she sat down to talk with me. There wasn't anything for me to say in my defense. I was a despicable cad, in every sense of the word.

The words she said hit me like a hammer. "Mike, I want a divorce. I have spent most of my life with your miserable disposition and your grudges. You've made my existence a living hell most of the time. I have endured it because I loved you and thought that you loved me in spite of how you treated me. I realize now that I've just been kidding myself. There is something very basic missing in you, and while I feel sorry for you, I won't subject myself or these children to you any longer.

"God knows, with Kathy, my burden is hard enough, and Mike, I just can't carry you any longer. If you will take my advice, you will seek out God and let Him help you become a man who can look at himself in the mirror again. I will be praying for you, as I have done since the first day I met you."

Then she heaped some burning coals on my head when she said, "I have to ask you to forgive me for the harsh words I said to you this morning. I really don't want anything for you except the best. If I hadn't been beside myself with anger, I would never have said what I did. Believe me, I want only the best for you."

When we went to bed that night, I lay there for quite a while contemplating what I had done. It reminded me of a small boy who has built a castle out of blocks and yet he can't resist the urge to turn around and kick the whole thing down. Why was I like this? What had happened to the rabbi who was raised to love God before anything else? Why did I find it impossible to forgive Him for the misfortunes in my life? This unforgiveness in my soul was now going to cost me my wife and children.

Betty lay beside me, but she might as well have been a million miles away. I could have reached out and touched her, but I knew it would do no good, for she had withdrawn herself from me. I had no one. I was alone. The arrogant stubborn man was reduced to a lost child again.

I finally fell into a deep sleep, from which I was aroused some time later by a feeling that someone was in the room. I sat up in bed and looked over at Betty. She was fast asleep. The hands on the luminous dial on the bedside clock showed a few minutes after two. Then I looked to my left, and there, standing in a soft glow, was a figure with His hands outstretched toward me.

I could feel my heart begin to pound, as fright washed over me. Then the figure spoke my name.

"Michael, Michael."

I was too frightened to answer.

He spoke again. *"Michael, Michael."*

This time I swallowed and asked, "What do You want?"

With a soft voice that contained all the compassion of the ages, all the love that any man could ever require, and all the gentleness of a mother holding her first-born child, He said, "Why do you hate Me?"

The frightened man, the arrogant man, was still in charge. "Hate You? I don't even know who the heck You are."

The figure vanished. He was gone, and I was once again alone. Completely alone.

I found myself in a cold sweat, trembling, and shaking. I also seemed to be unable to stop sobbing. I glanced over at Betty, and she was still in a sound sleep, so I slipped out of the bed and began to wander through the house. I went from room to room, trying to get away from the turmoil that filled every fiber of my being. Peace. My God, how I wanted to feel some measure of peace.

Hours went by, in which I felt like my very soul was being scourged. The faint light of dawn was beginning to filter through the drapes when I found myself in the den. I cast my eyes over the bookcase, looking for something to read, something to occupy my mind.

My eyes lit upon the little Hebrew New Testament that I had received so many years ago. My hand seemed drawn to it by a force I couldn't explain. I took it down from its perch on the highest shelf and began to leaf through it.

Then it seemed that an even deeper stillness began to fill the house. I could no longer hear the ticking of the clock. The ever-whirring motor of the refrigerator ceased its steady sound, and a silent hush that filled me with expectancy came over the room.

The only sound that existed on this earth was the faint rustle of the pages of the Bible as they finally came to rest. They were open at the Gospel of John, and as I looked upon the pages, the 24th and 25th verses of the 20th chapter seemed to leap out at me:

> But Thomas, one of the twelve, called Didymus, was not with them when Jesus came.
>
> The other disciples therefore said unto him, We have seen the Lord. But he said unto them, Except I shall see in his hands the print of the nails, and put my finger into the print of the nails, and thrust my hand into his side, I will not believe.

The knowledge, the realization, the recognition of Him who had stood by my bed and asked that agonizing question, "Why do you hate Me?" floated over me like a tidal wave.

The nail prints in his hands. Oh, my God! That glowing figure that had stood at the side of my bed had had the nail prints in His hands. I remembered seeing them, and the mark upon His side.

The exaltation that filled my soul was too much to ever describe. I had not only found my God again, but my Messiah as well. I could feel the unhappiness, the bitterness, the arrogance begin to flow out of my body like a steady stream, while a surging river began to fill me with peace, hope, steadiness, and love. Yes, love. I was going through a baptism of love.

I fell to my knees and gave Christ my life. I was truly being born again. It was a new man who uttered the words of profession, "You are my Savior, my Messiah, and my God."

13

ROME, the eternal city, with its beautiful antiquities, marvelous fountains, and its unbelievable drivers. I leave this city with the vague impression that the twentieth century has somehow infringed on another age. It is a city that has survived the best and the worst of man in order to remain a monument to civilization.

Everyone on the tour is still agog over the many sights they have seen — the Forum, the Colosseum, Vatican City, with its beautiful Sistine Chapel. It isn't hard to imagine that if the cars were replaced by horses and chariots and all of the Coca Cola signs vanished, we would all be back in ancient Rome.

We are now on our way to Athens, Greece, which is one of the last stops before Israel. The best of the trip is yet to come, but I think we all feel the spirit of adventure and that this journey will have a lasting effect on all of our lives.

Rome has a beautiful airport, which is named, appropriately, the Leonardo da Vinci Airport. We have arrived in the midst of throngs of Italians who are shouting greetings at each other, with arms waving in all the gestures that it takes for an Italian to communicate. As I thread my way through the happy throng of people, I discover that I have lost Betty. I look around and scan the crowd for a glimpse of her, but she's nowhere in sight. We are all soon looking for her, but still no Betty.

I feel the panic begin to rise in me as I hurry through the crowd, looking frantically left and right. Finally I see her behind one of the barricades, and they won't let her in because I have her passport. After the difficulty is ironed out, and I have my wife with me again, I begin to relax.

As we rise higher and higher into the blue Italian skies, I reflect on the last time I thought Betty was lost to me, some nine years ago. It had taken an act of God to return her to me then. I will never forget her face when I woke her that morning, and told her I had accepted the Lord Jesus Christ as my Savior.

It was beautiful to watch the look of disbelief slowly turn to wonder as I poured out the story of my marvelous meeting with Jesus. I found myself saying, "Honey, you *have* to forgive me, because I have to have a chance to be the man you want me to be with the help of Jesus. I've tried for years to make it by myself, but I've been much too mixed-up a person to be able to do the right thing on my own." It was then, after all those years of marriage, that Betty heard for the first time that I had been a rabbi who had turned completely away from God because of my brother's death.

It may sound strange that this secret existed after so many years, but that shows how deep my feeling of rejection had gone. The freedom I was now feeling was over-whelming. We began to discuss what course we should take now, and what we thought Jesus would want me to do.

The first thing I wanted to do was to start going to church. Betty had wheedled me into taking her to the local Presbyterian church a couple of times, for their Christmas Eve service, so this church was the logical place for us to go. There was another reason also. The minister, Dr. Donald Gard, had given off such a glow of love that I knew he was the man I wanted for my pastor.

That same morning found me at the Presbyterian church telling Dr. Gard what had happened in my life. I told him that I wanted to stand up before God and the congregation and affirm my faith in Jesus Christ and accept Him as my Savior.

It had to be truly a leading from the Lord that sent me to this man. He was so kind, and I knew from our first meeting that he really cared for me and what happened to my life. His was the first hand of Christian fellowship that was held out to me with all the love of Christ behind it.

I know how important this was to me, because if I had met someone who had shown skepticism about my conversion experience, it would have hurt the seed that had been planted in me. Fortunately for me, Don was a man who watered that seed and gave me the TLC that I so badly needed.

Sunday morning found Betty and me once again standing before a congregation, joining a Presbyterian church, but what a difference from the last time! This time I was fairly delirious with happiness. I wanted to shout at the people sitting in the pews, "Do you know how lucky you are? You've had the chance to know Jesus your whole lives."

One of the first things I noticed about having Jesus in my life was the change in some of my attitudes. The day after I joined the church, I was in the office, without any request from the stewardship committee, making out a pledge card for my tithe. There was no red pencil with a smart-aleck remark this time. Instead, I deemed it a privilege to give back to God a portion of what He was giving to me.

Tuesday found me talking to a member of the Christian education committee, telling him of my extensive background in the Old Testament. I offered to teach any classes in which he could use me, and I soon started with a class of fourth-grade children.

Betty and I joined the Mariners, too. This social organization within the church proved to be one of our biggest blessings. Through it, we met people who became our dearest friends. Many of them played important roles in future events in our lives. I will never be able to thank all of these wonderful people enough, because they so totally accepted me and made me feel like I was one of them.

I have to be honest and tell you that I was afraid that I would be hit with some anti-Semitism. Of course, I didn't still believe that the Christians would drink my blood, as I was taught when a child, but I did believe a lot of them hated Jews. I was prepared for this eventuality, but I need not have been afraid, for these people treated me with true Christian love. In fact, they went out of their way to make me feel part of the church.

Not long after I joined the church, I started to feel a terrific inadequacy about my knowledge of the New Testament. Although I had read it through a couple of times in conjunction with a commentary, this only served to let me know how much I didn't know. The New Testament is the fulfillment of the Old Testament which opened the door wide for me, and I wanted to know the New as well as I did the Old.

I went to see Don about my problem, and he suggested that I start attending the Lay Academy. This was taught through the presbytery for members of the synod who wanted advanced teaching on the New Testament.

Don, who was a PhD, and had been a professor at Princeton, taught most of the classes. Thus started a new routine of learning such as I hadn't had since Hebrew school. I felt fortunate that I had all the knowledge that I did, for it helped me immeasurably to acquire the in-depth understanding that I wanted of the Scriptures.

I can't explain to you how much better life became after I met the Lord. A whole new world had opened up for me. The Presbyterian church seemed a symbol of everything that was new and good, and I gave my all in working in it. One of the proudest days of my life was about a year later when I was ordained a deacon. I will never understand why some men have to be begged to accept office in the church. I deemed it the greatest privilege when I was asked, and my only hesitancy was whether I was worthy of the job or not.

In the meantime, another wonderful event was taking place. Betty and I were going to become parents again. When Betty came home from the obstetrician and told me this news, I told her that for someone who had accepted the fact that we couldn't have any children, she was sure putting up one heck of a fight. We were now going to have four children, the oldest only five.

All during Betty's pregnancy, I kept saying one thing: "It's got to be a boy, because I want to name him after Don." I don't know why this was important to me, but it was. Maybe I wanted to show Don in a tangible way how much I loved him.

The day of the birth was upon me before I knew it, and I went into my usual routine of falling to pieces. This time Betty had quietly asked one of our friends to be with me, so I would be kept out of her way as much as possible.

I still don't know how I managed it, but I had myself *and* my buddy both in the labor room. He was in nearly as bad a condition as I was. We were each holding on to one of Betty's hands, while she tried to reassure us that everything was going to be okay.

With a big sigh of relief, Betty sent the two of us to the expectant fathers' room when she was ready for the delivery room.

When the doctor came out and told me the baby had been born, and my wife was in good condition, he found two of us with our fingernails bit down to the knuckles. It took me a couple of minutes to realize that the doctor hadn't told me whether the baby was a boy or a girl.

I ran after him, demanding to know what I had, but he wouldn't tell me. He said, "Betty wants to tell you herself." I knew then that we had another little girl, and Betty was going to break it to me gently. For her sake, I tried to look as happy as possible when I saw them wheeling her out of the delivery room.

Betty was lying on her stomach, a little pale from the ordeal she had been through. I leaned down and kissed her and told her how happy I was with my new daughter. She just looked at me a moment, then she said, "What am I going to have to do, send little Don Gard back where he came from?"

I can't tell you how thrilled I was. I told Betty over and over what a good job she had done. She knew I couldn't wait to tell everyone the news, so she told me to get going. I kissed her and thanked her again for my son; then I was off like a town crier, telling everyone about my boy.

When I came back that evening to see Betty, she was in an odd mood. Everytime she looked at me, she cracked up laughing. Finally I got her to tell me what was so hilarious. She told me, "Mike, I don't know for sure whether he was serious or not, but while I was in the delivery room, Dr. Araujo made a statement that struck me so funny that I can't quit laughing about it." Dr. Araujo had delivered all of our babies, and he had never seemed to be a man who was that funny, so I was curious about what he had said.

Betty said he sounded quite serious when he announced, "Betty, *you* can have more children." She started giggling and said, "But then he gave a big sigh and said, '*But* Mike can't have any more. I just can't go through it with him again.'"

I must have looked pretty sheepish by this time, because Betty stopped laughing, put her arms around my neck, and told me she loved me for caring so much. It helped me for her to do this, because once again, after it was all over with, I had felt like a fool.

It was a proud and happy day in our lives a couple of months later when Don baptized Donnie in front of the congregation. In my heart at the moment, this child was dedicated to God. I knew Donnie would have a ministry that would be a glory to his Maker. Little did I know how soon this would prove true.

Now began a deeper and deeper involvement in the church. In 1965, I was ordained an elder, and I began to serve on the various committees in the session, becoming involved in different aspects of the presbytery and synod.

About this time, Don accepted the pastorate of a church in the East. This made me very unhappy, because he had been my best friend and mentor. The Reverend Earl Mason, who had been the assistant pastor, became interim pastor, and I became head of the stewardship committee. I soon found out how hard a job it was.

As part of the pastoral seeking committee, I helped bring our new senior pastor, Dr. Ralph Didier, to the church. Then I became the head elder of the church, which had a membership of about 2,500, and in 1968 I was president of the church. I had also been nominated for vice president of the United Presbyterian men of the synod of Southern California.

Slowly but surely, the many posts I held in the Presbyterian church began to go to my head. The humility that I had found when I met my Lord face to face was beginning to fade away.

Every Sunday I wore the beautiful black robe with the accompanying stole, as I assisted the pastor with the worship service. I gave the call to worship, the invocation, and finally I read the Old Testament Scripture for the day.

Standing opposite the pastor in my pulpit, I began to think I was really something special. The members of the church were such nice people, and they went out of their way to let me know I was appreciated. After the service was over, and Dr. Didier was standing at one door while I was standing at another, the people would file by, shake my hand, and many would comment, "Mike, no one reads the Scripture like you do. You make it come alive."

Pride and arrogance invaded my spirit, and before long, I was beginning to take all the glory, honor, and praise from God, for myself.

Betty, of course, was well-aware of the change that was going on within me, and was distressed with the results. She was seeing the reincarnation of a man she thought dead, a man she had been happy to bury.

I was so important, I was convinced that the church would find it impossible to survive if I missed even one of its meetings. During one period of time, I had been at a meeting every night for six weeks without a break. This activity was causing quite a strain in my marriage.

Then Betty received an alarming phone call one morning. It was from one of our dearest friends, and she was in terrible condition. In between sobs, she managed to tell Betty what was wrong.

Her fourteen-year-old son, with the help of another boy, had decided to try his hand at purse snatching. The boys had spotted a likely victim and had made a run for the woman, each going on a different side of her to cause confusion while they made a grab for her purse. Everything worked according to plan — except for one detail. As the boys sped by her, the lady was thrown off-balance, and fell, hitting her head as she went down. She was killed instantly, and the two boys were being held, among other charges, for first-degree murder.

When Betty hung up the phone, the Lord was already

dealing with her. She was under conviction for the shallowness of her faith. She hadn't had the words to comfort her friend, and she also realized that she didn't have enough depth to her faith to give her own kids the help they would need to keep a terrible thing like this from happening in their lives. When I arrived home that evening, Betty filled me in about our friends and ended with, "Mike, if you feel your faith is deep enough, that's your problem. I'm going to start searching for more of God. There must be more than what I've got."

As usual, when your back is against the wall, the Lord has been busy building a way out if you'll just look for it. Well, Betty started looking. She remembered some of the words she had been hearing from another friend, Alyson Fry.

A group of us who had met through the Mariners were holding meetings once a month where we read and discussed the Bible. For the past few meetings, Alyson had been bugging us all. She had been going to some meetings at a church called Christian Center, and she had had some wonderful new experience that was really drawing her closer to the Lord. She tried to hold her enthusiasm down so she wouldn't scare us all off, but enough showed through that Betty remembered it now that she herself felt the pressing need for a closer walk with the Lord.

After a short discussion with me, when I told her I didn't care what she did, Betty called our troubled friend and asked her to go the next day to a prayer meeting at Christian Center with her. She told her she knew she needed help, and maybe some could be found at this meeting.

It's hard to tell you about the woman I came home to the next evening. It was like someone had lit her fuse. Her first words were, "Mike, I've never seen or heard anything like this meeting in my life." She said, "Those people knew who they were praying to! They were praying with so much belief that their prayers were going to be answered that they were thanking Him before He even had a chance to answer." She went on, "I have never been around that much faith in my life. I'm so tired of praying to the thin air. I want what those people have. I want to *know* who I'm talking to, like they do."

She chattered on about miracles of healing she had seen, miracles to which people had testified, and how the pastor had impressed her with his sincerity. She and her friend had gone to see Pastor Wilkerson after the meeting, and he had prayed with them and had promised to go see the two boys at the jail.

My thoughts were mixed. I was glad that Betty had been able to get help for our friend, but I sure didn't want her to turn into a ding-a-ling like Alyson. Alyson was so far gone that our friend and pastor, Earl Mason, was asking her if she was climbing the glory pole.

Betty was saying something about going to a meeting at Christian Center next Sunday night, and I found myself saying that I would go, just to get her off my back. I figured I could manage to keep her feet on the ground. Besides, she had aroused my curiosity about the big attraction at this place.

Sunday night found us scrambling for a seat in a packed church. I looked around me, impressed at the caliber of people crowding into the pews. I expected a lot of dowdy people, more or less the dregs of society. But these people were all nicely dressed, well-groomed people, whose only claim to looking "different" was that they all looked happy. I never saw so many happy faces in church in my life.

The service began, and I felt a variety of emotions. I loved the singing. The songs weren't the traditional hymns that I was used to, but many of them, which the people all seemed to know, were Scripture set to music. I saw people all around me with their hands held up to the Lord in praise. I could feel myself tighten up, because I was feeling too many emotions, and I wasn't able to handle them all. I could feel the tears begin to rise in my eyes, and I wasn't sure I wasn't going to make a spectacle of myself.

The pastor didn't speak about any philosophies; there was no *Reader's Digest,* no *Time* magazine—just Jesus and Him crucified. After the sermon, which I really enjoyed because Pastor Wilkerson taught right out of the Bible, I found it hard to control myself. The pastor faced the congregation and invited those in the audience who wanted more of Jesus to come forward. The choir began to sing softly, "Just as I am, without one plea—O Lamb of God, I come, I come!"

People all around me began to leave their seats. Quietly and reverently, they moved forward to accept more from their Jesus. How I yearned to go with them! But I was president of one of the most prominent local churches. How could I go forward announcing to the world that I needed more of Jesus? My pride and arrogance won out, and I sat through the altar call with my knuckles turning white from the grip I had on my seat.

Betty continued to go to Christian Center every chance she got. I didn't know it at the time, but she had everyone from the prayer meeting busy praying for me, because I was getting more and more out of hand. My rebellious nature was starting to manifest itself again in many ways.

One day all of this confusion came to a climax. Betty had been at Alyson's and she had prayed for a real born-again experience and had asked for the Baptism in the Holy Spirit. She didn't have to tell me. All I had to do was look at her face when she walked into the house. There was a look of joy, of love, and a radiance about her countenance that couldn't be misunderstood.

I could feel the harshness and the uncompromising stubbornness begin to rise in me. I knew that she had received the Baptism in the Holy Spirit with its accompanying speaking in tongues. I was mad, clear through. If she thought I was going to live with this stupidity, she had another think coming.

With a heart full of malice and resentment, I packed my clothes and left home. I didn't tell Betty where I was going; I had decided I was never going to come back.

I began driving toward Florida. The fermenting blend of spite, grudge, animosity, and guilt was the fuel that kept me going all the way to Miami. I arrived in the middle of a hurricane, the perfect complement for the virulent brew steeping inside of me.

I had finally reached my goal. Freedom. In Miami, I found myself a motel room where I could be comfortable until I could make firmer arrangements. There were no encumbrances, no responsibilities, and I was free.

As I sat in my room, I began to wonder, "Free for what? To be lonely? To have no one who cares whether I live or die? Free to become a bitter old man?" For the first time, the enormity of what I had done began to dawn on me. I was like a man who was slowly beginning to wake from a terrible nightmare. Even though it was my own creation, it was still a nightmare.

The face of my little boy, Donnie, as he stood on the curb waving bye-bye to his daddy, swam in front of my eyes. My God, what had I done? Betty had stood beside me through all these years. How on earth could I justify what I'd done to her now? I knew there must be complete chaos at home. Here I was again, with my life in a million pieces, and as usual, it was I who had smashed it to the floor. Thus began a night filled with regret, remorse, and then wonder whether there was anything I could say or do to compensate my family for the failure I had been as a husband and father.

The next morning I mustered up enough courage to call home. I looked at my watch as the phone began to ring and realized it was only 6:00 A.M. California time. After a few rings, Betty's voice came over the line with a sleepy hello.

I finally squeaked out a "Hello, honey, it's Mike. Will you talk to me?" After a small pause, I heard a calm, "Of course I'll talk to you."

I told Betty where I was, and what my thoughts had been all night long. Then I took a deep breath and asked her if I could come home. Without a moment's hesitation, she said, "Yes. It's your home, you know, Mike, and it will always be here for you." I told her I would be back as fast as I could make it.

When I hung up, I sat there for a minute trying to fathom what had happened. How come Betty was so calm? She sounded like I'd just made a trip to the corner store. I had expected to spend the first fifteen minutes trying to quiet down a hysterical woman—

I must have broken most cross-country records on my way back, harboring an underlying fear that Betty would change her mind. It was about six o'clock in the evening when I arrived in Anaheim. As I walked up to the door, my son John ran out to play, shouting a greeting, "Hi, Dad" as he went by. My daughter Laurie was watching cartoons on TV. She looked up and said, "Hello, Daddy," and went back to her TV. I walked into the kitchen where Betty was busy fixing supper. She gave me a kiss and said, "Supper will be ready in a minute, honey. Why don't you go freshen up."

I walked back to the bedroom in a daze. Where was the chaos? Why wasn't everyone crying and screaming? Where were all the high emotions? Didn't they realize the prodigal son was back? After the children were put to bed, I learned what had transpired at home after I left.

The first few days were pretty bad for Betty, but she tried

her best to stay on top of it for the children's sake. She had gotten a baby-sitter and gone down to take over our business. This kept her pretty busy, but when she had a chance to think, she would call Alyson, and Alyson would pray with her. It was these prayers and Christ that kept her going.

Alyson told her that she would have to praise the Lord that this had happened, because He must have a plan even though she wasn't able to see it. Betty said, "I kept telling God, 'I'm praising You for this even though I don't mean it. It's up to You to make me mean it, because I'll not stop until You do.' "

Betty had told the children that I had gone to visit my brother. To keep them from looking into my closet, and finding everything gone, she had taken the doorknobs off so the door couldn't be opened. This was why the children were unconcerned. They never knew they nearly lost their daddy.

As for Betty, she told me that the same night I had arrived in Miami, and had gone through that terrible night, she had had a marvelous experience with the Lord. She told me, "I had gone to bed for the night after I had prayed for quite a while. The fear and sorrow over what had happened was still with me, and I couldn't seem to escape from it. Once again I got up and went down on my knees by my bed and prayed to my Lord.

"I told Him that He had to take this burden from me, that I could no longer carry it. I committed you, Mike, to Him and told Him I was willing to praise Him from this day forward even if I never saw you again. At this moment, the peace that passeth all understanding began to wash over me. It was like being in the eye of a hurricane. It didn't matter what was going on in the periphery of my life. I was at peace in the center. It was Jesus and me, and He was more than enough.

"I climbed back in bed, and one by one during the night, each of the children crept in bed with me. I was lying there half-asleep, holding my kids and praising the Lord for the total peace He had given me, when the phone rang. I knew before I picked up the receiver that it was you calling, so I guess I telegraphed this peace across the country to you."

Betty didn't mention the Baptism in the Holy Spirit, and neither did I. I knew that Betty was praying in tongues at times, but I didn't talk about it. We had reached an unspoken agreement that we would try to get along together, but there would be some subjects that would be taboo.

I attended Christian Center with Betty most Sunday evenings, because I enjoyed the service as much as she did. Before long, Pastor Wilkerson asked me to teach an adult Bible class in the Old Testament on Sunday morning. I told the pastor I would have to see how it would work out, as I was already teaching an adult class at the Presbyterian church.

About this time, Betty asked me to take her to a Full Gospel Business Men's meeting at the Disneyland Hotel. I told her that I would much rather take her out for a nice dinner and to a movie. She begged and pleaded with me to take her to the meeting, because a man that she had read quite a bit about was the speaker. His name was Harald Bredesen. I told her that I didn't want to hear some guy give his testimony. Needless to say, I found myself at the meeting at the Disneyland Hotel.

The banquet hall was packed, and as we threaded our way among the tables, I was wondering what the heck I was doing here.

We finally spotted our friends who were holding seats for us, so we sat down to eat and await the program.

Harald Bredesen proved to be a very good speaker. He gave a warm and moving testimony of his encounter with the Lord and of his experience with the Baptism in the

Holy Spirit. This experience seemed to mean so much to him that he had me intrigued. I had never given Betty much of a chance to tell me how she felt about it, but as I was more or less a captive audience, I had to listen to what this man had to relate.

When he had finished his talk, there came the usual altar call. I didn't think I would have to go through one of these outside of church, but here it was again. There was one small difference this time, however. I couldn't stay in my seat. I don't know how it happened. One moment I was sitting at the table toying with my coffee cup, and the next moment I was standing with many others in front of the whole gathering in response to the altar call.

After a few minutes, we were all herded into a *prayer* room like a bunch of cattle. Pastor Wilkerson stood at the door. He asked me if I had come forward for the Baptism in the Holy Spirit. To cover my ignorance, I inquired facetiously, "Is it free?" When he answered yes, I said, "Then I'll take it." Now I was committed to hear what these men had to say.

One of the pastors stood and began to speak. "The primary reason for receiving the Holy Spirit into manifestation is to give us power for abundant living. This spiritual blessing is your legal right according to the command given on the Day of Pentecost, Acts 2:38–39.

"In the Scriptures, there are also other reasons given why we should receive the Holy Spirit. It gives the power for Christian service, Christian witnessing, and Christian living.

"Now the pastors and counselors will move among you to pray with you for the Baptism in the Holy Spirit."

14

I WOULD like to be able to say that I yielded my heart at this time and believed that I could receive the miracle, but I was still in the grip of the spirit of unbelief. I could not escape from the doubt that this Baptism in the Holy Spirit was in the psychological realm instead of the spiritual realm.

I was acquainted with many people who were supposed to have received the Baptism in the Holy Spirit, but I thought they might have all been psyched-out.

One of the latest to experience this blessing was our assistant pastor at the Presbyterian church, the Reverend Earl Mason. He was the pastor who had asked Alyson if she was climbing the glory pole.

The Lord had worked in Earl's life, through Betty. One day I came home from work and found her in a complete turmoil. I wanted to know what was wrong, and her answer left me even more puzzled.

She said that the Lord had been telling her since early that morning to call Earl's wife, Harriet, and ask her to go with her to the Thursday morning prayer meeting at Christian Center. It was already Wednesday.

Betty didn't want to make the call. She knew how Earl felt about all this *emotionalism,* and as far as she knew,

Harriet probably agreed with her husband. Thursday was also Earl's day off, and Betty couldn't imagine Harriet going with *her* to church on *his* day off.

At eleven o'clock that night, when we were already in bed, Betty threw off the covers and with a disgusted tone in her voice said, "All right. All right. I'll call, but I'm not going to beg. I'll ask her just once, and it's up to You to make her answer yes."

I wasn't sure to whom Betty was talking, but I *was* sure she had flipped her lid. She stomped into the living room, and I could hear her dialing the telephone. The inaudible conversation lasted only a minute.

Betty walked back into the bedroom with a look of amazement on her face. She said, "As soon as Harriet answered the phone, I blurted out, 'Harriet, will you go with me to the prayer service at Christian Center tomorrow morning?'" Betty paused as if to remember accurately. Then she continued, "There wasn't even a moment's hesitation before Harriet answered, 'It's Earl's day off tomorrow, and I never go anywhere on Earl's day off. What time do you want me to pick you up?'"

Betty was a nervous wreck waiting for Harriet to come by for her the next morning, because she was convinced the Lord was beginning to deal in Harriet's life. You can imagine Betty's surprise when she saw Earl sitting in the car ready to go with the two women.

His first words to Betty as she climbed into the car were, "How long does this thing last?" Betty told him it was usually a couple of hours, to which he retorted, "Well, let's sit in the back so I can leave whenever I want to."

At the supper table that night, Betty told me what had happened. She said, "Mike, that same overwhelming feeling of love swept over Earl as it did me on my first morning at Christian Center. His eyes filled with tears, and you could almost see the Lord wrap him in His arms."

What has happened to this man after that prayer meeting is a testimony to God. There have been hardships and sorrows, but most of all glory, because God has been with him every step of the way.

Now I was getting ready to ask for the same experience that had seemed to pour strength into the lives of so many people I knew, and yet the persistent doubt was there. Was this a valid experience, or was it something they had all talked themselves into? Was this something that happened only 2,000 years ago on the Day of Pentecost when 3,000 people were filled with the Spirit after Peter preached to them, or was it for today?

The ministers and personal workers were now moving among the people. They were beginning to lay hands on them and to pray for the infilling of the Holy Spirit. I heard one person after another lapse softly into a tongue I couldn't understand.

I began to pray quietly for the faith that I would need to have if this was to be a genuine experience. I knew it would take a miracle for this stiff-necked Jew to truly believe.

While I was deep in prayer, I realized that Pastor Wilkerson was standing in front of me, ready to pray for me to receive the gift of the Holy Spirit.

He prayed fervently for me, but I seemed unable to release the faith that I knew was so small.

Several of the other pastors prayed for me also, plus many of the personal workers. I continued to sit in that chair, and before I knew it, it was two and a half hours later. I don't know what made me persist so long.

I was beginning to get tired and not just a little bit sorry that I had walked into this room in the first place. I was just about ready to get up to leave when I felt a hand on my shoulder.

It was the youth pastor at Christian Center, Jene Wilson, who is now the director of Teen Challenge here in Orange

County. He began to pray for me to receive the Baptism in the Holy Spirit.

But I decided I had had enough. I thought, "These people are not going to let up on me until they think I have received." I decided to fool them, to take things into my own hands by speaking in Hebrew, Aramaic, Arabic, and Chaldean.

Jene still had his hands upon me praying when I took a deep breath and started speaking "in another tongue"; in fact I started speaking in several tongues.

The men who were near us could hear me, and they started thanking God and praising the Lord that I had received.

I could feel my very soul shrink inside of me. They were so sincere, and I was such a phony. I had fooled them all, but I hadn't fooled myself and God. We both knew what a despicable act I had just perpetrated.

Then Jesus in His mercy looked down on me and performed the miracle I needed to give me the faith I needed.

The voice that I had heard five years before came through the lips of Jene Wilson. Once again, all sound save this voice was lost to me. There was again quiet all around me, and only the sound of *His* words filtered through this silence into my heart.

"Michael, Michael, worship Me in a new language." That was all, but that was enough. That He cared for this disobedient, doubting Thomas the way that He did, was a beautiful miracle then and is still a wondrous one today.

I opened my mouth and forgot my intellect. I forgot all my languages. The only language that I used and wanted to use was the heavenly language that Jesus seemed to be pouring into me until it came out like a babbling brook full of joy, and beauty, and love.

I don't know how it sounded to others, but to me it was the final release to a soul that had been kept in captivity since its birth. I felt like a bottle of champagne that had been shook and shook its whole life, and now the cork had been popped, and the sparkling liquid was bubbling out, full of life and happiness.

I knew I wouldn't have to be bottled up anymore to slowly go flat and sour.

I have seen so many Christians relegate their lives to this existence. Now with the Baptism in the Holy Spirit, my life could be like a well of living water, always full and always ready to quench another's thirst.

When I emerged from that prayer room, I was like a baby chick who had worked with his beak, pecking and pecking until there was a hole big enough in his shell that he could finally come out. I felt like all my feathers had been fluffed.

And I was ready to go out and do the Lord's work, whatever it would be.

Betty could tell that a miracle had occurred when she took the first look at me. She keeps saying it's the mouth. That's where the Holy Spirit shows. She says when a person is full of the Holy Spirit, his mouth is soft, with smile lines all around and a gentleness that doesn't escape the eye. Anyway, she just walked up and threw her arms around me, and started to praise the Lord.

Betty said I kept waking her up all that night because I continued to praise God in the new language He had given me.

I was reminiscing over the many years I had lived without being conscious of the many times Jesus had touched my life preparing me for this day.

I remembered back to my childhood during public school and that time of assembly. There was one hymn in particular that used to flood me with peace every time I heard it.

It was "Come, Thou Almighty King." It was my favorite, and every time we sang it, I would feel such a love in my heart that I could hardly bear it.

As I lay there, I began singing the melody, using the new language the Lord had given me for the words. It was funny how this song was so deep in my memory. I remembered another time that Jesus had gotten through to me with this beautiful hymn.

While I was still in the service, I hurried off the post one Sunday. I had a date in town, and I was late. As I passed by the Quonset hut that served as the base chapel, I was stopped by the sound of a familiar hymn. Once again, "Come, Thou Almighty King" was calling to me.

It was like a finger beckoning me to come in and join the worshipers. I must have lost all sense of time, because before I knew it, I was sitting inside, listening to the sermon, and my engagement in town was forgotten.

After the service was over, the chaplain came over to me and asked me what a nice Jewish boy like me was doing in a place like that.

I told him something about my background, especially about my training in the Old Testament. He was a real nice guy, and after taking me to lunch, he asked me if I would consider reading the Old Testament lesson to his congregation each Sunday.

I can't remember now if I considered this a challenge or a privilege or what, but the following Sunday found me standing before a Protestant congregation, reading from the Old Testament.

It wasn't long before I was approached by the Catholic priest who wanted me to help him during Mass by reading from the Old Testament to his people. After a few weeks, I was doing double duty every Sunday, serving these two congregations.

It didn't take the post rabbi long to get wind of my extracurricular activities. He cornered me one Sunday and said, "Mike, we also have the Old Testament you know, so how about helping me with *our* service?" There was no way out. There went the rest of my Sunday morning.

As I lay in bed, that time and many others began to tiptoe through my mind. I know now that the Holy Spirit was revealing the many times He had been present in my life, dropping tiny seeds on very rocky ground.

I could see that this stubborn Irish girl who was sleeping beside me was the focal point of His plan. She had been with me for years, slowly chipping away the many layers of hardened stone that I called my heart.

I was open again, like a newborn baby, ready to learn all the Lord wanted to teach me.

It had been a glorious moment when I was born-again, when I had felt the actual presence of the Lord for the first time, but this Baptism in the Holy Spirit was the icing on the cake.

POWER. I felt the power of the Lord for the first time. The power to fill a person's life with peace when there is a storm raging all around him. The power to fill a person with joy when there is sadness all around him. The power to fill a man with love when there is hate all around him, and most of all, the power and the boldness to witness to the world about the glory of the Son of God.

My days began to take on new meaning. Before, the people with whom I came in contact every day had been a challenge to me; now, they were people I could tell all about Jesus.

For years I had been a salesman, and I had been pretty good at my trade, which was, in reality, selling myself. Before you can sell your product—whether it be draperies, which was my business, or a used car—you have first to sell yourself.

Now I found I had to quit selling myself. I had to sell

Jesus Christ. People had to see Him in my life before any words that I said about Him could ring true. This is the hardest job any Christian can have, and it is one that we all must face.

God wants us to be like Jesus, and that goes against the natural man. After much thought, I concluded, *"I could never be justified in any action I committed that was NOT Christlike, no matter what the circumstances were."* In a nutshell, this is what is expected of us.

I have not been able to live up to that understanding, but I have stopped rationalizing about the many times I failed to abide by it. Admitting I am wrong frees me to ask for forgiveness and become right again.

I was now beginning to feel out of place at the Presbyterian church. My emotions were so mixed that I knew I could never make a decision one way or another about leaving, so I gave this completely to the Lord. I just wanted to do His will, not my own.

I was still deeply involved with every aspect of the church. I loved the church and its people dearly. They had always been more than good to me. These wonderful Presbyterians had taken me to their hearts. It made me feel like the most wretched ingrate that I was even thinking about leaving, yet something was making me consider this move. The Presbyterian church is a liberal church, and with my background, I couldn't have been more fundamental in my belief.

Many of the events that Betty was seeing for the first time at Christian Center were common to my background. I had seen my father lay hands on people for healing and to bless them since I was a child. I had seen many miracles and believed in them with all my heart.

I believed the Bible was literally true. I not only believed that the whale swallowed Jonah; if it had said Jonah swallowed the whale, I would have believed that, too.

One morning I had just finished making a sale, and was driving to my next appointment, when a deep silence seemed to invade the car. I pulled to the curb and began to pray.

All around me I could feel the brooding presence of the Lord. I was frightened and aware that He seemed to be commiserating with me. Melancholy and sadness enveloped me, and I began to weep. I didn't know what was wrong, so I started the car and drove to our store as fast as I could.

Betty was there. She was sitting at the desk, deep in thought. She didn't even realize I had walked in.

As I approached the desk, she glanced up with surprise written across her face. I must have looked pretty forlorn, because her first words were, "What's wrong?"

Those words opened a floodgate, and between tears I was finally able to blubber out what had happened to me that morning in the car.

Betty didn't seem surprised now. In fact, she seemed to know exactly what was going on. Now she really was beginning to upset me because she started to laugh.

I guess I was starting to look pretty disgruntled, because she straightened herself up and said, "Sorry, honey, I was laughing at myself, not you. I know what's wrong with you. Let me tell you how the Lord was dealing with me at the same time He was dealing with you."

Betty continued, "As I was driving to the store this morning all of a sudden these words were being fed into my mind, 'It is time to leave the Presbyterian church.' My immediate reaction was, 'How in the world am I going to tell Mike? He loves that church so much.'

"When I got to the store, I called Alyson and told her

what had happened, and we discussed how I was going to tell you. We finally decided that I would feed you an extra-good supper, and after I put the children to bed, I would sit down and tell you."

Betty was shaking her head as she said, "I forgot all about the Lord maybe having plans of His own to tell you Himself. I also forgot that He always sends a confirmation when He tells us something."

I, of course, knew this was what the Lord was trying to get through my thick skull, so I said, "Let's write our letter of resignation right now." We both prayed that the Lord would give us the words, and ten minutes later the letter was signed, sealed, and mailed.

15

WE ARE now approaching Athens, Greece. I know that beneath us are many lovely little islands peeping their heads above the beautiful blue Aegean Sea. It is dark, but the faint specks of lights that you see occasionally let you know that the islands are there, ready to delight the tourist.

It will be late when we set down in Athens, and everyone will be tired. Already most of us are beginning to feel the extra strain that travel tends to impose upon the body.

When the plane rolls to a stop, I look around for my son, John, and my daughter, Laurie, who is being treated like a little princess. She is nine years old, going on forty, and she loves to be one of the crowd.

Laurie sits on my lap during the bus ride to our hotel. She wants to know if her doll, Athena, came from Athens. John is cuddled next to his mother, bravely trying to stay awake so he can take in all these new sights, but he is fast losing his battle with the sandman.

The whole group is fed and assigned to their rooms. John and Laurie are well on their way to dreamland, and Betty and I are taking a short walk toward town before we call it a day.

As we amble down the street, we see many of our group.

Betty points out a couple walking arm and arm ahead of us. The woman's head is on the man's shoulder. In the faint light from the shop windows, I recognize Irvine and Edna Harrison.

Dr. Harrison and I are the co-leaders on this tour, and I have never met a man I admire more. He is a totally dedicated Christian, one whom I would like to emulate.

Betty remarks about the example that Irvine and Edna have given to us all of the solidness of a good Christian marriage. These two have been married thirty-eight years and are still much in love.

Fatigue begins to walk hand and hand with Betty and me, so we head back to our hotel for some much-needed sleep. The children are fast asleep, and I am glad that Betty had overruled me and made them go to bed instead of out with us for a walk.

Betty and I fall into bed like a couple of rookies who've been on a forty-mile hike, and we're both asleep instantly.

About one in the morning, the shrill ring of the telephone brings Betty staggering to her feet. In a fog, I hear her answer the phone, and then I hear alarm come into her voice. Betty shakes me wide-awake. I hear her say, "That was Edna. Irvine must be having a heart attack!"

I get out of the bed like a shot and am grabbing for my pants while Betty tries to quiet the children and get them back in bed. As I run out the door, I yell at Betty to start praying.

Taking the stairs two at a time, I feel panic begin to rise and take over. "Lord, God, stand with me now so I can help" is my prayer as I approach the Harrisons' room.

There is an instant response to my knock, and Edna shows me to the bathroom, where Irvine is sitting. There is no doubt that he is in terrible trouble.

I telephone Betty and tell her to call Dr. Brandenburg, who is on the tour with us, and Don Pierotti. "Get them here as fast as you can!" I can hear myself yelling. Betty says, "Okay, Mike, take it easy. Everything is in God's hands."

Her steadiness has a calming effect on me, and I turn to Irvine as I hang up the phone.

His face is etched with pain, his breath coming in short gasps. He is holding his chest, barely able to speak. I lean over him and ask, "Irvine, have you taken your nitroglycerine?" I hear a barely discernible *no*.

Edna gets his pill for me, and Irvine manages to get it down. I sit back on my haunches, holding his hand, waiting for the pill to take effect.

In a matter of minutes, there comes one last audible breath, and Irvine falls over into my arms. I don't know whether he is unconscious or dead. At this moment, Dr. Brandenburg and Don Pierotti burst into the room.

The three of us get Irvine stretched out on the hard bathroom floor. Don Pierotti gives mouth-to-mouth resuscitation, and Dr. Brandenburg massages Irvine's chest. Betty arrives, and Dr. Brandenburg tells her to go to the lobby to get medical help. "We have to have adrenalin," he tells her. On her way, Betty stops and tells Allene Wilkerson, Pastor Wilkerson's wife, what is happening. Allene goes to be with Edna.

In the lobby, Betty finds no one around who knows what to do. The manager calls for an ambulance, but he says it will probably take a while for it to arrive.

Betty calls the local hospitals, asking for a cardiac specialist. She can find no one who speaks English. She tries to tell them that she needs adrenalin, but they don't understand.

Finally Betty calls the American Consulate. The official to whom she talks doesn't speak Greek, so he can't make himself understood any better than she can. He keeps her on the line for a good fifteen minutes while he calls here and there for information. Finally, he comes back on the line advising her to wait for the ambulance.

Betty is on the thin edge of hysteria as a Greek couple comes into the hotel. A clerk tells them what is happening, and the woman tells Betty that she speaks English, and asks if she can be of any help.

Betty grabs her like a drowning person grabs a lifeline. She asks her to tell the hospital that we need adrenalin, that we have a doctor who can administer it.

At this moment, the husband of the Greek woman tells her that he doesn't want her to get involved. He takes her by the arm and forces her into the elevator, leaving Betty standing in a state of shock.

An hour has gone by since the ring of the telephone jarred us into this nightmare.

In the Harrisons' room, Dr. Brandenburg is keeping Irvine's heart beating by pressing rhythmically on his chest, and Don Pierotti continues to give mouth-to-mouth resuscitation.

Both men are dripping with perspiration. Their knees are in agony. They have been kneeling on the marble bathroom floor for nearly an hour.

Everyone knows, especially Dr. Brandenburg, that it is useless, but no one is willing to give up. They continue on, not willing to let go, no matter what their intellect tells them.

Mahlon McCourry and I have been praying, reading the Psalms aloud, crying out to God to perform a miracle. Everyone on the tour has been interceding for Dr. Harrison.

I look up from my Bible to see Betty come through the door. The men with the ambulance are on their way up by the stairs, as the European elevators are not large enough to accommodate the men and their stretcher.

As I watch the Greek ambulance men and Dr. Brandenburg work to get Irvine on the stretcher, I realize these are almost battlefield conditions compared to what we have come to expect at home when there is an emergency.

The stretcher is made of two poles with a piece of canvas slung between them. There is no adrenalin, no resuscitator, just a small bottle of oxygen and a mask that they try to put on Irvine's face.

Dr. Brandenburg tries to explain that the oxygen will do no good, because Irvine isn't breathing. The men grab the ends of the stretcher and start down the stairs. At each landing, Dr. Brandenburg makes them put Irvine down for a moment, while he massages Irvine's chest and Don breathes for him.

We finally get the stretcher into the ambulance. Dr. Brandenburg and Don get inside. I turn to Mahlon to tell him to watch over the group; then I get in a cab and follow the ambulance to the hospital.

When we arrive at the hospital, we find them taking Irvine into the emergency room. I leave Edna with Allene Wilkerson, Barbara Firms, and Linda Proctor, who came in the cab with us, and go into the emergency room.

The Greek doctors have taken over. They are hooking Irvine up to an EKG machine, and the doctor calls for adrenalin. I watch the scope on the heart machine. There is just a straight line across the middle of it. No heart activity at all.

The doctor shoots the adrenalin into the heart; then he begins to pound on Irvine's chest. As long as he pounds, the lines on the scope show some peaks, but as soon as he stops, the line becomes straight again. They repeat this procedure, but with no more success than the first time.

Finally the doctor looks up and shrugs his shoulders in the universal gesture of "It's no use." I watch him as he folds away his instruments. After two hours of the most intense endeavor, the struggle is over.

I can't accept this finality—those two men in that hotel

room working to the point of exhaustion; the people on the tour still on their knees, not knowing that it's all over, praying and beseeching God to return this man. These make me refuse to accept the fact that the end has come.

I take the authority granted unto me by the Lord Jesus Christ. I hear myself saying, with a boldness that I don't possess, "In the name of Jesus Christ, Irvine, I command your spirit to come back to your body."

The stillness in the room is a hushed expectancy; I know that God is going to move. I can feel Him all around me. I just have to believe enough to see this miracle.

In an even louder, more bold voice, in a triumph of belief that comes from the very depth of my soul, I shout, "Father, in the name of Your Son Jesus Christ, I command this spirit to come back into this body!"

There is movement. I know that Irvine is here again. I can't have been mistaken. With my own heart pounding like it is going to leap from my chest, I lean closer and gaze upon Irvine's face.

There is a faint flutter of his eyelids, then slowly, ever so slowly, his eyes open. But these eyes are different; these eyes have beheld God, and in an instant, even before the slight shake of his head back and forth indicating NO, I know that Irvine is with his Master, and he doesn't want to come back.

Yes, Irvine is healed in the most perfect healing of all. He is where we all want to be. Where there is love, peace, joy—and the Lord that he has loved his whole life.

This is his day of triumph. The day when he will be able to present his many crowns to his God. The crowns he has stored in heaven by his faithful service to Jesus Christ.

I stand by Irvine's side as he peacefully goes to be with his Maker, and I rejoice for him.

As I walk out of the emergency room, I know that God will have to give me the strength to minister to Edna. I tell her what has happened, but I don't think she can hear me. She's in a state of shock, so I don't try to talk any more. I'll tell her about it later.

As we ride back to the hotel in the cab, I glance down at myself. I realize that all I have on is a pair of pants. No shirt, no socks, just a pair of pants.

Now that the state of emergency is over, and the high emotional strain begins to subside, I shiver with cold. I know it isn't cold outside, but every shred of heat has left my body. I know this is shock setting in, and I'm glad I'm going back to Betty and the children.

When I open the door to our hotel room, I see my family sitting there, wide-awake, waiting for me. Betty tells me they have been praying ever since we left for the hospital.

I say to my children, "Kids, Dr. Harrison has gone to be with the Lord." Then, with the simple faith that only children seem to possess, my son John remarks, "Gee, isn't he lucky?"

Betty and I smile at each other over the heads of our children. Then we all go to our beds. As I lay there, much too full of the strain of the night to fall asleep, the memory of another night steals across my mind. I guess it is John's remark that is triggering these thoughts, because this was also his reaction on that cold December night in 1968.

It was a week before Christmas, and Southern California was having one of its rare cold spells. In prior years, the children had complained about the balmy weather, saying, "It doesn't seem like Christmas with the sun shining so brightly." This year was different. It was cold, and there was enough of a nip in the air to satisfy any youngster who was longing to greet Santa with a little of the North Pole.

Betty and our children were piled in the bed in our bedroom watching the Christmas specials on TV, while I was sitting in the dining room working on the Sunday school lesson I would be teaching the following Sunday in the Christian Center.

I was hard-pressed to knuckle down to work this evening. I could hear the children laughing with their mother, and I wanted to be with them, enjoying the shows.

The Christmas tree in the corner of the living room blinked its lights, beckoning my admiration of its tinsel beauty. I had never seen such an array of gifts as the ones that were nudging each other for room under the garlanded Christmas tree.

These things were distracting me from the job at hand. With a sigh of self-pity, I returned my thoughts to the notes in front of me, and I was soon engrossed in the lesson.

Suddenly there was a flash of lights, and I looked up with a start to see a spark coming from an electrical wall outlet in the living room.

The sheer draperies that were hung in front of the outlet billowed out in flames, which promptly raced to the Christmas tree in the corner.

The tree seemed to explode right in front of my eyes. This all happened in a couple of seconds, but it seemed like a lifetime as each new horror crowded its way on top of the other ones.

I was having a hard time comprehending what was happening. Fires happen to other people, not me. They are something you read about in your morning paper. You shake your head over some other poor fellow's tragedy as you drink your coffee, safe and secure in your own world.

When the first shock of what I was seeing passed over me, I started yelling for Betty.

She and John came on the run down the hall. Betty took one look at the inferno that was our living room, and ran out the front door for the hose. I heard her yell at John to turn on the water.

I rushed into the kitchen for water, but the screams of my children in the bedroom quickly brought me to the back of the house.

I found my girls screaming with fear, and I grabbed them both. As I ran from the room, I spotted the dog cowering in the corner, so I made a lunge for her. With two children and a dog in my arms, I plowed through the hall, which was already in flames, and got them out the back door through the kitchen.

By this time, the house was plunged into utter darkness, black billowing smoke pouring out of every window. The panes of glass were bursting, one by one, as intense heat built up in the house. It was as if the very fires of hell had reached up to engulf us.

Betty and I met around the corner of the house. She kept saying that she couldn't get back in with the hose, that the fire went too fast.

I told her I was just grateful she had gotten out with the boys, that putting the fire out was the firemen's job.

"Mike, what do you mean, boys? John was the only one who came out with me."

Stark terror must have been mirrored on our faces. We both started to call frantically for Donnie. One of our neighbors had seen a little boy running up the street.

This gave us a momentary hope that Donnie was out of the house, but this hope faded fast as Donnie failed to materialize.

When Betty realized that Donnie was in the house, it took the brute strength of three people to hold her from going back after him.

The fire department had arrived, and Donnie was their first concern. I told them where we had seen him last, and I shoved Betty into the arms of one of my neighbors.

Even above the screech of the sirens and the roar of the

fire, Betty's cry for her baby sent chills down my spine. As I raced around the back of the house with the firemen, I yelled back, "No matter what, don't let her go!"

The window of our bedroom hadn't blown out yet, so we broke it. The draperies were on fire, and I started yanking them out, unaware of pain as the flames licked at my hands.

The fire became more intense, forcing us back. Smoke as black as night continued to pour out of the house, and I didn't need the firemen to tell me that if Donnie was in the house, there was no way he could be alive.

I knew I had to go around to the front of the house and tell Betty that Donnie was gone. I moved to her side with leaden feet, praying the most fervent of prayers—that God would meet her need.

When I reached her, she said, "Our baby is with the Lord." There was no more fight in her, no more struggle, just a surrender to something that was so far from her understanding that she would never really be able to comprehend it. She would accept it, she would praise the Lord, but she would never understand why. Even more important, she would never ask why.

Our neighbor, Barbara Marshall, was standing with Betty. The three of us found ourselves on our knees on the cold wet grass, thanking God for the knowledge of where our baby was, even though the firemen hadn't found him. We knew where he was, and that he was already totally safe.

The firemen found Donnie's body much later. The Lord was good in this instance, too. Betty was already in the home of our next-door neighbor with our children. I was still at our house, and when the fireman came out carrying Donnie, he walked right by me, telling me that he had found him.

I didn't see him or hear him. The only reason I know that

it happened is because he told me about it the next day.

The Lord blinded my eyes and stopped up my ears, so that my memory of Donnie is of a laughing, curly-topped little boy who was as tough as they come. He will never be a pathetic little bundle lost in the arms of a big fireman. I praise the Lord for this.

Pastor Wilkerson was one of the first people to arrive at the Ericksons' home next-door. Roy and Shirley had thrown open their door to us all. They had just lost their son, Mark, a few months before from leukemia. He was the same age as Donnie, so I knew how fresh their own wounds had to be.

Pastor started praying with us, and the full awareness of where Donnie was came upon the three of us all at once. Pastor, Betty, and I stood in the middle of the room laughing with pure heavenly joy as this reality burst forth.

I could just see those fat little legs marching right up to Jesus and climbing on His lap. I knew those baby arms were around the Lord's neck, and his tousled head was nestled under His chin. What more could a father want for his son?

Friends were beginning to pour in from all over. Many of our Presbyterian friends were the first to arrive. Gene and Jody Brewer came. Jody took the shoes off her feet and put them on Betty's.

Dr. Bob Curtis came. He was the children's pediatrician. At midnight he went to an all-night drugstore in a neighboring town to get prescriptions filled for Kathy's anti-convulsive medicines.

Betty's mother and father arrived. They were in bad condition, but when they saw the faith of their daughter, they had to stand.

A phone call was placed to Betty's sister who was living in Hawaii. Betty talked to her sister, and told her that we were praising the Lord. Joan couldn't believe the words she was hearing. She said she was on her way by the first plane she could get.

Then Betty went into the bedroom where our children had been since the start of the fire. Shirley Erickson had gotten them inside the house as fast as possible so they would not have to see any more than necessary.

Betty took her father with her to tell our children that their brother was gone. I don't know what kind of reaction she expected to get, but I doubt if it was the one she got.

John and Laurie were jealous. That's right, they were pea green, they were so jealous. "How come Donnie gets to go with the Lord? Why don't we get to go?" Here were two children, six and eight, and they had a truer sense of what it's all about than most of us adults. To them, to be with Jesus made Donnie the luckiest boy who ever existed.

Laurie even pointed out that God had made sure Donnie's playmate Mark was already in heaven waiting for him. What could be neater?

Later that night, when Betty told me how the children had taken the death of their brother, the realization of the power of Jesus to make the difference swept over me.

I remembered what it had been like for me when my brother died. I had been a raw, exposed nerve, aching, hurting, lashing out at the injustice of it all. There had been no Christ to stand between me and the agony of loss.

It was not only the loss of my brother that had assailed me; it was the fact that David hadn't had anyone to die for his sins. There was no one to plead his case before his God. I knew that as a Jew, David would be judged, and there would be no one else to pay his fine.

John, who loved his brother as I loved mine, had the comfort of knowing that Donnie was in the arms of love in its purest form. He knew Jesus had reached down and had taken Donnie with Him to be one of the children of heaven.

A couple of years later, John wrote a composition for Memorial Day about his brother:

My Memorial Day Story

My Memorial story is about my baby brother, Donnie. Me and Donnie were great pals. He would always do the same thing that I did. When I watched TV, he would watch it with me. He would sleep with me at night. I was in the top bunk, and he was in the bottom bunk.

It was about Christmastime when my brother was lost in a fire in our house. I miss him very much, but I know that he's up in heaven with Jesus. Donnie was a swell brother, and I loved him very much.

I praise the Lord, and thank Him very much for letting me have a brother like Donnie.

John Esses

We finally went to Glen and Alyson Fry's home that night. Dr. Becker, a friend of ours, had come by and given us some pills so we would go to sleep right away. We took them, but neither of us was able to relax enough to let them do their job.

Betty and I lay there, not saying much to each other. What was there left to say? We knew that we had many hard days ahead of us, and I knew there would be times when we would feel like we were drowning in despair.

As humans, we have to mourn, but as Christians, we do not mourn as those with no hope. Betty summed it up a couple of days later when she was talking with Dr. Didier, who had come by on a condolence call.

Dr. Didier said to Betty, "You will have a few weeks of despair before this wound begins to heal." Betty answered him with, "No, Dr. Didier, I'll not have weeks of despair. I'll only have moments until I get hold of God again."

Dawn came the next morning without either of us having slept. We knew the day would require the making of many decisions. God was very good to us, because He had a message for us the first thing that morning, one that helped us face the trials of the first day without our youngest son.

Barbara Marshall, who had knelt the night before with Betty and me in prayer, had already come by the Fry's with a message she had received for us from the Lord.

It was side-marked with the date 12/18/68, received at 11:55 P.M.

It was with grateful hearts that we read the message from our God, who knew Himself the agony of losing a Son:

Oh, my grieving children
Turn to Me as you weep.
Let Me carry your sorrow
Your loss is great for you
    at this time.
This is as it should be.

Out of all this chaos
You shall reap a rich harvest
    for My vineyard.
Through this suffering, you shall
    see great rewards
In Me, Your Strength and Redeemer.

Continue in Me, My children.
Thou shalt be blessed beyond
    measure.

I, the Lord, taketh away.
I also give.
Rest assured your loved one is
    with Me and never suffered pain.

As you weep, My children,
Breathe in Me and breathe out your
    anguish — your suffering.
Stay near Me, so that I can
    comfort you and sustain you.
Through this hour of need,
    turn to Me — your Savior.

Remember, I love you.
I care for you.
I am your Rock — your Redeemer.
Through Me thou shalt be
    blessed among all men.
Your service for Me has just begun.

I love you!
Keep My commandments!
I am always with you.
I will never let you down.
I love you, My children.
I am at your beck and call.

Of all the words the Lord gave us to comfort us, the ones
I needed most were, "Rest assured your loved one is with
Me and never suffered pain."

I knew Donnie had been terribly burned, and this was a
horror that I couldn't remove from my thoughts. As much
as my mind would try to flee from thinking about it, the
thought would keep creeping back in. Then despair and
agony would hit me like a solid blow to the solar plexus.

Later that day, I received a call from the coroner of Orange County. He told me, "Mike, rest assured your boy never suffered any pain. He was dead from carbon monoxide poisoning within a minute and a half. The flames did not reach him until he was already with your Jesus. He just went peacefully asleep and woke up with the Lord."

The Lord's message made it easier to face the day. I decided to go ahead with my business, because I knew customers were depending on me to get their draperies in before Christmas. Besides, I desperately needed to keep occupied.

I didn't realize it at the time, but my working also served as a witness to the keeping power of the Lord. Whether I was at the workroom where the draperies were made, or at the store where our business neighbors could see the Lord sustaining, or in the office where I was installing the draperies, everyone who was expecting me to collapse at any moment actually saw the power of the Lord. He was holding me in the palm of His hand.

At noon on the day Donnie went to live with Jesus, I was at the store picking up some parts I needed. As I was walking out, Norman Hahn, a brother from Christian Center, walked in.

Norman had come by to express his deep sorrow over my loss, and to see if there was anything he could do for me. Before he left, he told me that he was on his way to see Don Pierotti in the hospital.

"What's wrong with Don?" I asked. After Norman had filled me in, I said, "Let's go in the back of the store and pray for Don." During our prayer, I was overwhelmed with the knowledge, This is what it's all about!

As we knelt in the quiet room, I silently sought the Lord's guidance as to how to pray, and suddenly I was praying aloud with a boldness that surprised us both, for complete and perfect healing, for the doctors to be confounded and for the surgeon's knives to be bound.

The assurance that the prayer was being answered (and indeed it was, I learned later) swept over me like a tide that could not be denied. I knew what God wanted of me. He wanted me on my knees, praying and ministering to and for his people.

The words that I had uttered as a Bar Mitzvah came to me again with a crashing reality: "I will follow in the footsteps of my forefathers and illuminate the word of God to His people."

I knew then that my life had to be dedicated totally to Jesus and His ministry.

16

PASTOR Wilkerson had asked Betty and me what kind of service we wanted for Donnie's funeral. Our answer came from the knowledge that many people would be attending that funeral who were not born-again, dear friends of ours who still did not know their Savior personally.

I said, "Pastor, preach a message on salvation. I want them to see Jesus." We had already decided on the songs: "How Great Thou Art" and "It Is Well with My Soul." Betty and I knew where our boy was, and we wanted those attending to be as aware of this as we were.

On the way to the chapel, I leaned over to Betty and said, "Do you realize Donnie is the first Esses who was a Christian when he went to meet his Maker?" Of all those who had gone on to meet their God, Donnie was the only one who had known Him while he was still with us. One of Donnie's first words was Jesus.

The chapel was packed, and the sermon so moving and full of hope that I could feel Jesus walking down the aisles ready to meet the souls who were turned toward Him. Many people came to us afterward saying that they had never attended such a funeral—one that was totally uplifting, one where they could see the parents were praising the Lord.

130

I reflected upon what it would have been like if I had still been an Orthodox Jew. I would have had to sit on the floor for seven days. I would have torn my clothes; I wouldn't shave for thirty days. I would have cried, and wailed, and mourned as one with no hope, because without Jesus there would have been no hope.

I thanked God with all my heart and soul that He had sent His Son to prepare a way for my son. For I knew that no matter how hard I tried, I could never be the father that Donnie had now. He was going to be raised to be the person he was supposed to be without the mistakes that a human parent is bound to make. Yes, my son was a very fortunate boy. Praise the Lord.

God was not through showing us love and compassion. We were still totally enveloped in His grace. When He said He would never let us down, He meant it.

The momentum of the events that follow a fire and a death catches you up, and suddenly, it sits you down. Dawn of a new day arrives, and you look around you and wonder, What now?

Everything was gone. The house, furniture, clothes — the accumulation of years of living — all gone in a moment's time. Inevitably, the practical everyday problems have to be faced. But we didn't have to face them. Jesus faced them for us through His people.

We didn't know where we were going to go from the Fry's home, but neighbors of ours in the real estate business presented us with keys to a house in Garden Grove, with instructions to stay there until our home was rebuilt.

Saturday afternoon, after the funeral, we went over to have a look at our temporary home. The sight that met our eyes was hard to believe.

Every room was completely furnished. There were TVs, beds, chests, chairs, rugs, and lamps. There was a couch, a dinette set; the kitchen was completely equipped, down to the can opener. There were toasters, electric coffeepots, waffle irons, steam irons—every appliance that's made.

In the living room, Save-On Drug had sent a tree which was set up and decorated, with all kinds of presents under it for the children.

The closets were jammed with clothes, some from people we'll never know, and some from department stores that had been kind enough to meet our needs.

There were sheets, towels, blankets, pillows, pillowcases, and food. You could never believe how much food! It was in every cupboard, on every shelf, and behind every door. There were cases piled to the ceiling, containing every kind of canned goods available to man.

The whole sight was overwhelming. The storehouse of heaven had been tipped over, and it had all poured into our laps. The graciousness of God and the goodness of His people were a miracle to behold.

With grateful hearts, we brought our children to this house, and began to put our lives together again.

I was very proud of Betty. As hard as it is for a father to lose a child, it can be even more devastating for a mother. Donnie was still a toddler, so Betty was with him all the time, loving, teaching, and caring for him. He was her baby, and I knew his loss had left a terrible void in her life.

A scant month after Donnie's death, the Lord eased the pain in her heart. She told the story to me when I returned from church on a Sunday morning in January. "I awakened from a dream early in the morning," she said. "It was the first time I had dreamed of Donnie since the fire. In the dream, he was alive and well, playing with his sisters and brother."

The dream was so real that Betty felt she could reach out and touch Donnie, and the loss of her baby was unbearable to her when she had to wake up and face the reality of his death.

She continued, "I got out of bed and wandered through the house, looking everywhere for some kind of solace. I went to the children's room, but they were all still sound asleep. The sight of their sleep-smudged faces should have helped me; instead, it made me long for my baby even more.

"I felt he should have been there, too, nestled down in the bed where I could tiptoe over and tuck the covers around him as I was doing for his brother and sisters."

When she left the room, a sorrow that she had not felt since the moment of his death descended upon her, and she could hear her very soul begin to groan in agony.

Betty found herself on her knees, telling God that if He was who she thought He was, and if Donnie was really with Him, He had to make it real to her now. Right now. She couldn't wait. She told Him that if she had to feel this kind of sorrow any longer, she couldn't bear to live.

With shaking knees, she walked into the kitchen, and for an unexplainable reason, she reached over and turned on the TV.

Betty said, "When the television came to life, it was with the words, 'Let us pray,' written across the screen. Then the voice of the minister came over the air, and I felt that God was holding me in His arms, saying, 'Now, now, Mother. I've got your chick, and you're not to worry about him.' "

The prayer was one of standing still and knowing He is God, and it was more than enough to drive away the sorrow and the grief that had her in its clutches.

With a voice full of gratitude, Betty went on: "I felt my prayer had been answered in such a beautiful way, and I was relieved of the terrible pain in my heart. What happened next was more than I had ever hoped for.

"God reached down to this sparrow and let me know that this prayer was just for me, because the announcer came on the TV with these words: 'The meditation this morning was given by Dr. Donald Gard of the First Presbyterian Church of Anaheim, California.' "

Betty was crying by this time, telling me between tears how God had had Don Gard pray for her while she was grieving for her baby who bore the same name.

Later that morning, Betty called Don and told him what had happened. He told her that it had been three years since he had taped that prayer. In fact, he had taped it the year Donnie was born.

A studio technician had pulled a tape and played it in Los Angeles five minutes after a mother in Anaheim prayed for some sign that God was real. The timing was exactly right, and the minister was the godfather of the child who had died. Some may call that a coincidence; I call it a miracle.

17

IT'S MORNING here in Athens. I didn't sleep last night, but I seem to be functioning well, considering everything.

I know everyone will be wondering what is going to happen now. I'm so grateful that Allene Wilkerson came with us at the last minute, because she's going to fly back home with Edna.

I see the work of the Lord in her decision to make the trip. He knew how badly she would be needed to take care of Edna.

Betty and I have decided to continue on the tour. This is what Irvine had come for, to show these people where Jesus and His followers had walked. We decided that it was a tribute to him to continue, Betty taking one group while I took the other.

It was with a great sense of loss that our small caravan started out to walk where the apostle Paul had preached in Athens. As we climbed to the top of Mars Hill, we looked out over the city. What a story these ruins could tell if they could speak!

My thoughts turned to last year at this time when I had stood on this same spot with Irvine while he read from Acts 17:22–31. It was now my turn to stand in front of God's people and preach this sermon from God's Word.

I remembered back to that moment on my knees praying for Don Pierotti when God made it real to me that I was to become a preacher. A short time later, I talked to Pastor Wilkerson and asked to be enrolled in the intern program at Christian Center.

During Christian Center's second Charismatic Clinic, I was asked to teach at Melodyland, a large theater-in-the-round opposite Disneyland in Anaheim.

Little did I know that Pastor Wilkerson was going to be given the vision that this huge place was the perfect new home for Christian Center. When I heard this news, I must admit that I thought it was impossible.

My problem was that I was a newcomer in a ministry that was obedient to the move of the Holy Spirit, and one which expected God to perform His miracles.

It was not without a great deal of opposition that Melodyland Christian Center came into being. I at first was reminded of Don Quixote when I looked at Ralph Wilkerson. I thought if ever there was an "impossible dream," this was surely it.

Every conceivable barrier was put in this man's way. First of all, the price was astronomical. Second, the City Council was not sold on the idea of a church in this location. Third, the hotel and motel neighbors of Melodyland were up in arms at the thought. Fourth, the existing tenants were raising Cain, because they didn't want to vacate.

With most men, this would have been too many hurdles. But Pastor Wilkerson had God's promise, and he stood on it. And at Easter, 1970, Melodyland became Melodyland Christian Center, a tribute to a God who performs miracles, and to a man to whom He gave faith to be His instrument.

On August 23, 1970, I was ordained to the ministry before approximately 3,000 people attending the third annual Charismatic Clinic.

Pastor Wilkerson was the speaker who gave the charge to the men who were being ordained this night. I can't remember all he said, but the one point that really sunk in was that I was on God's team now. He said that I couldn't play for the crowd, only for the Lord.

More than anything on earth, I wanted to serve Jesus, and make Him proud of me, so I placed these words in a special pocket in my heart. For this time, I was not kneeling to please my father who wanted an unbroken line of rabbis. This time, I was kneeling to please Jesus who had died for me.

Life now became a total joy to me. I was teaching and preaching constantly. It began locally, but I was soon going further and further from home base.

"Melodyland School of the Bible" had come into existence through Pastor Wilkerson. This was a school for lay people who wanted a deeper knowledge of the Word. It was based wholly on the Bible. I became a teacher in this school, and I found the greatest pleasure in making the Old Testament come alive to my students.

There is so much of Jesus in the Old Testament! I don't see how the Jews' eyes, including my own, could be so blind that we could not see that 333 prophecies concerning Christ in the Old Testament were gloriously fulfilled in the New Testament.

When I was speaking at the University of Oregon, I was told that two of their computer scientists had run this problem through the computer. The odds against *one* man fulfilling these 333 prophecies were 67 to the tenth power, a figure so astronomical that it approaches infinity. What an answer for the intellectual inquiring about the validity of Jesus!

During the early days of my ministry, there were meetings in Sacramento with Pat Boone, Full Gospel Business

Men's meetings in Indiana, Pennsylvania; San Diego, California; Rome, Italy; Santa Monica, California; Milwaukee, Wisconsin; Pittsburgh, Pennsylvania; Palm Springs, California; Chicago, Illinois. . . .

I spoke at many charismatic conferences. There were conferences in Toronto, Canada, at the University of Pittsburgh, Trinity church in Sacramento, San Jose, California, Eugene, Oregon, and many, many others.

This schedule included many one-night stands, and of course, my heavy weekly commitment to Melodyland. There was no time left for my family.

My life was starting to blur from one meeting to the other. I was gone on Betty's birthday. I wasn't able to attend the children's annual Christmas play. I was gone New Year's Eve. The straw that broke the camel's back for Betty was my daughter Laurie's birthday, January seventeenth.

Laurie was sitting on the floor, surrounded by little girl friends, opening up her birthday presents. Suddenly, with no warning, she ran from the room crying bitterly that her daddy wasn't there. Nothing Betty could say or do consoled her.

When I came home, it was to a very angry wife. I told her she must realize that I had to do the Lord's work, and all these places needed me. Who else was going to be able to bring the Old Testament to the people like I could?

Betty wouldn't listen to reason. She said foolish things like, "You're not the only evangelist available, but you are the only father Laurie has." Then she went on with, "God knew you had a family when He called you into His service. If you listen to Him, He'll send you where He wants you to go, and He'll provide time for your family, too."

I just couldn't see it. There were all those people needing me. How could I disappoint them? In fact, I had one of my most important meetings coming up, in Mexico City with many of the leading speakers from across the country attending.

The following Thursday was a very busy day. I went to the morning service at Melodyland, then I taught my afternoon class. That night, when I finally got home, I wasn't feeling too well.

I attributed this to many things. I knew I had been overdoing, but I was trusting the Lord to uphold me. After all, I was doing my utmost for Him.

Another thing that was preying a little bit on my mind was a note that our friend Arlena Grubb from Corona had given to me. Arlena said that the Lord had given her a prophecy for me a few days earlier, while she was in prayer:

January 29, 1971 — Michael, hear the word at My mouth. There was a father with many sons, who owned much land. To his younger and beloved son, He said, "You will one day inherit a portion of these vineyards along with your brothers. Take this small vineyard now, that you may learn how to care for it, against the day that I give you your whole inheritance."

The son had much to learn; and in his inexperience and neglect, the young plants faltered. Some grew wild and produced only bitter fruit. Others withered on the vine for lack of water. In the end, the vineyard became a wilderness.

The vineyard is your family, and you are the husbandman. I set before you a small field, that you might learn to be faithful in obedience to the working of it. The young plants whom I entrusted to you need the pruning of discipline, the nourishment of My love through you, and the water of the Word.

Listen well, younger son. I am attempting to mature

you for larger vineyards. Learn the task at hand so that you will be prepared for the coming tide which will come against all my vineyards and husbandmen.

I desire your love and obedience. Move with me now, for the time grows shorter.

My love is toward you.

That this might really have come from the Lord instead of from Arlena's fruitful imagination crossed my mind, but I swept that thought away swiftly with a protestation of how much good I was doing and how much I was needed.

As the evening wore on, I became more and more uncomfortable, having some pain in my left wrist, and also in my chest. It was difficult for me to get a deep breath.

I wasn't doing too good a job of masking my distress, and Betty asked if she should call our doctor.

"Don't be silly," I told her. "I'm just having some gas pains." It was soon evident that it might be more than this, however, so I gave in and let her call Dr. Wyatt.

He told me to come to the emergency room at Anaheim Memorial Hospital. I was really reluctant to go, but Betty kept insisting that it was better to be sure that nothing was wrong, instead of just hoping.

Because it was late, and all our children were in bed, I drove myself to the hospital. I considered just riding around for a while, then going home, but I was afraid that Pete Wyatt would call Betty and ask where I was.

I approached the hospital with an air of unconcern; after all, the Lord was on my side. He knew how badly I would be needed in Mexico City. I was going to be the only completed Jew there. We are few and far between, and I knew the Lord was aware of it.

The pain that I had been experiencing had subsided somewhat, so I was sure that this whole trip to the emergency room was a wild-goose chase.

In spite of my protests that I was really quite all right, the doctor insisted on making sure. First he did a cardiogram, which was all right. Second, he had X rays taken, which were all right. Third, he drew blood for a battery of blood tests. This didn't prove to be all right.

Dr. Wyatt explained to me that when a heart is in trouble, and a coronary is on its way, the heart releases enzymes which show up in the blood. The blood tests indicated I was beginning to have a heart attack, and Pete wanted me in intensive care immediately.

My reaction was a flat no. I told Pete there was no way he was going to get me into that hospital.

I tried to explain that I was going to be leaving on Monday for Mexico City. I told him how indispensable I was to this meeting, but he wouldn't listen. He kept saying, "I have to check you into the hospital."

After a great deal of fruitless arguing, Pete gave up in disgust. He finally said, "Mike, before you walk out of here tonight, I want you to sign a release absolving the hospital and me of any responsibility for what happens to you."

As I stood there, the pain was slowly building again, but I refused to give in to it. I knew where I had to be on Monday, and it sure wasn't Anaheim Memorial Hospital. With the sure knowledge that I was the perfect overcomer, I scrawled my name across the bottom of the release.

On the drive back home, I began to plan on how I would handle Betty. First, I decided to take a codeine tablet so I could fool her into thinking there was no more pain.

As I drove up to the house, Betty ran out to the car. I had been gone a couple of hours, so she was really scared. I told her to calm down, that the doctor had said I was just too tired, and I was having some gas pains. I told her that I was lucky that I was going to Mexico where I could get some rest and relaxation.

When we went to bed that night, I felt just fine. The

codeine had done its work. Feeling no pain, I lay there in the dark grinning to myself, because I felt I had really won this battle. Unfortunately for me, I had also lost the war. The events of the next day proved it to me.

The next morning, Bob DeBlase and I went over to Dr. Harrison's house to fix a traverse cord on one of his drapery rods. As I left home, I kissed Betty good-bye, assuring her that I felt fine. When we drove away from the house, I turned to Bob and said, "You know, Bob, women are sure easy to fool. You've just got to give them a little sweet talk."

I admitted to him that I was still feeling pretty bad, but I knew it was just a matter of time before I would be on top of it.

Meanwhile, the woman who was so easily fooled was already on the phone to Dr. Wyatt. "Pete, Mike came back last night and said you diagnosed his pain as fatigue and that all he needed was some rest in Mexico City. Is this correct?"

Pete nearly came through the phone, he was so agitated. "*Rest!* He'll *rest in peace* if he goes to Mexico City. Now," he said, "seriously, Betty, Mike is having a heart attack, right now. If he goes to Mexico City with its high altitude, you will probably have to go and bring him back home."

Needless to say, Betty was not about to let me get away with my charade. It was a very nonchalant woman who called me at the Harrison's soon after my arrival.

Betty said, quite casually, "Mike, after you and Bob get through fixing that rod, and you kibitz awhile, would you do me a favor?" She continued, "Pete's office called, and they want to do one more blood test before you leave for Mexico. Will you guys drop by and have that done before you come home?"

Well, maybe I hadn't fooled Betty, but she did a beautiful

job on me. Like a lamb being led to the slaughter, I dropped by to have one more blood test.

Bob and I sauntered into the lab at the hospital, and I told them that Dr. Wyatt had ordered a blood test done on me. I gave the girl my name; then we sat down and waited for her to draw the blood.

Suddenly, out of the blue, and in front of Bob's astonished eyes, I was shoved into a wheelchair by an orderly, wheeled round the corner to I.C.U., stripped of my clothes, put to bed, hooked up to the heart monitor, and an I.V. tube was placed in my arm. This was so they would have quick access to my vein if they needed it.

In the meantime, Bob had made a hurried call to Betty telling her what was going on, and she was on her way to the hospital. When she arrived, she went to the office and signed me in, as pre-arranged. That was pretty slick. My only advice to any man who wants to fool his wife is, Forget it.

When Betty walked into my room, I was lying there a veritable caldron of emotions. I was mad. I was scared. I was in pain. I couldn't understand why the Lord was permitting this to happen, but I was still determined to go to Mexico on Monday.

In a very persuasive tone of voice Betty said, "Mike, please calm down and just rest. If you're still all right by Sunday, Pete will release you to go to Mexico. He doesn't know yet whether this is just a very mild disturbance or if it's more important than that. So just relax, and don't fight our wanting to take care of you."

I could feel the fight begin to drain out of me. I knew that I would be on that plane Monday, so in the meantime, I decided to take advantage of all this, and get some much-needed rest. Betty gave a sigh of relief as she saw me begin to quiet down.

All of this happened on Friday. That evening, Pastor Wilkerson came by. I was glad to see him, and have him pray for me. I told him several times that he was not to worry; I was going to be with him on the plane Monday.

When Pastor left that night, I lay there thinking how grateful I was to the Lord that He had given me a man that I could love and respect as much as I did Ralph Wilkerson. I remembered back to the night of Donnie's death, and the look of radiance on Ralph's face as he prayed with us.

Saturday went by with many visits from Betty and Bob. I was still feeling pretty well, not much pain, and I could see no reason why I would not be able to go to Mexico. When Ralph came by on Saturday, I reassured him again that I would be with him on Monday.

Sunday morning came, and I was on needles and pins waiting for Pete to come in to release me. When he arrived, he said, "Mike, I want you here one more day. If necessary, you can go to the airport from the hospital." I didn't like it, but there wasn't much I could do about it, so I settled down to wait.

Sunday afternoon, Grace Robley and Elizabeth Kitson came by. In I.C.U., only members of your immediate family or your minister are allowed to visit. The nurse made an exception to the rule when she was told that these two women had come all the way from San Diego to see me.

Grace and her husband Rob, who is a medical doctor, have a very beautiful ministry in San Diego. Approximately a thousand people a week go to their home, attending all sorts of meetings, mainly on the Christian family and how to live a life obedient to the Lord.

I had spoken at their home several times, and I have never seen such disciplined people. Grace and Rob had also attended my classes at Melodyland School of the Bible. We had become fast friends.

Grace exchanged the usual pleasantries with me. Then she said, "Mike, they only let us in for five minutes, so let me pray for you." As Grace began to pray, a stillness came over the room, and I guess this is when the Holy Spirit began to talk to her.

Grace didn't say anything at all to me, but as soon as she left me, she headed straight for a telephone to call Betty. "Betty, I have something to tell you. I have just been in to pray with Mike, and the Lord let me know that He is going to take Mike home."

Betty immediately began to protest. "Grace, you have to be wrong. He is doing fine, just fine. He's not going to go to Mexico like he's hoping, but he'll just be in the hospital a few more days."

Grace said, "Betty, I have never known anything more clearly. The Lord is going to take Mike home, unless you can change *His* mind."

Totally bewildered, Betty asked, "How in the world could I do that?"

Grace told her to call every place where I had spoken, everyone she knew, to ask them to start praying for "the resurrection power" for Mike. Grace herself was going back to San Diego to get everyone down there started on this prayer.

When Grace hung up, Betty said she sat down like she had been hit in the head. For the first time since I had complained about the pain Thursday night, she was scared.

If anyone else had said these words to her, she would have probably sloughed them off. But Betty knew Grace, and the close walk she had with the Lord. Betty couldn't ignore her.

For the next two hours, Betty was on the phone. She called every place she could remember me preaching. Sacramento, San Jose, Eugene, Pittsburgh, Chicago . . . She called Oral Roberts University. They told her they would put the prayer for "resurrection power" on a twenty-four-hour prayer chain.

Many other churches said they would be praying round the clock. Even some of the religious radio and television stations were alerted.

Betty came by Sunday evening to see me, and I was still all right. Pete had broken the news to me that I couldn't leave with Ralph the next day, but I was already planning to meet him in Mexico as soon as I was released.

Ralph had been in earlier, and I had assured him once again that he was going to see me in Mexico City.

I wondered why Betty seemed so nervous. Now that I was all calmed down, and taking things in my stride, she seemed to be falling apart. I figured her as a typical woman: they stand while the crisis is in progress, but they let down after it's over. I told her to go on home and get some rest.

Betty reluctantly left to go home, as I learned later, to spend the rest of the night on her knees praying for me.

That night, the roof caved in on me. I went so sour it was unbelievable. The pains in my chest started to be much more severe, and panic set in.

By the next day, events were crowding in on top of one another, and I was soon reduced to a quivering mass of humanity. I developed double pneumonia and blood poisoning. My veins collapsed, and the danger of clots in my arteries became imminent.

Dr. Wyatt was trying every antibiotic he could think of, but nothing was having any effect. My temperature was holding at around 106°, and I was hyperventilating. Days became one big nightmarish blur. I found myself stark naked, lying on an ice mattress. They cool these things down to 65°. It's hard to believe, but as cold as that thing was, I lay there and sweated.

Now the Lord began to get through to me. I was beginning to see the light. I remembered the charge Pastor Wilkerson gave me the day of my ordination – to play the game God's way and not to the crowd. I had tucked that message in a pocket of my heart, but Satan had picked my pocket.

I was being put through God's humbling process, having once again gotten too big for my britches. Because I was doing the preaching and teaching, it was hard for me to remember that it was God's ministry, not mine.

Betty was right. God gives you the ministry He wants you to have – if you will only listen to Him. No one is as important as I had become to myself, and the Lord was about ready to prove I wasn't indispensable.

Because I had diarrhea from the antibiotics, the nurses had to clean me and change me like an infant many times every day. Each time, I could hear the Lord say to me, "Will you take this humiliation and praise Me for it?" I told Him I would, and I did.

The days blended together. I knew Betty was there, but I wasn't able to focus in on her. The Lord had me in His own kiln, dealing with me, burning out more of the dross hour by hour.

Thursday morning arrived, and it was as if I was coming back from another planet. I looked around me, and for the first time in days, I was aware of my surroundings. I began to follow the nurses around with my eyes as they accomplished their morning duties.

It was a funny sensation. I was aware of them, but they didn't seem to know it. I heard one of the nurses tell the other, "You better call the Pastor's wife, because he's failing fast."

A short time later, Betty's face swam into view. I could see that she was crying, but I didn't know why. I was feeling so much better. Why was the look of agony stamped all over her face?

She kept saying, "Fight, Mike, for God's sake, fight. I can't go on if you give up. You've got to come home for

the kids and me—we need you too much for you to go."
By this time, she was sobbing hysterically. A nurse came
over and led her away.

In a few minutes, I looked up and saw Allen Porterfield.
He was the young minister from Melodyland who was
holding down the fort while the others were in Mexico.

Allen leaned over the bed and clasped my hand in his.
In a soft voice he said, "Can you hear me, Mike?" I tried
to tell him that I could, and I think he heard me, because
he started talking very intensely.

He said, "Mike, I'm going to claim the resurrection
power of Jesus Christ flowing through your body. Do you
understand me, Mike?" I nodded yes.

He said, "Do you understand that I'm going to bind
Satan and the friends of Job who are telling you to give
up?"

I nodded yes, again.

Then Allen began to pray the prayer that God had given
him to pray. As he prayed, I became more and more aware
of what had been happening. I hadn't been coming back to
life. I had been drifting into death, on a cloud of lethargy.
I hadn't been fighting at all. I was just being washed ashore
like a piece of flotsam.

As I watched Allen walk out the door, a feeling of panic
began to inundate me, and I began to hyper-ventilate again.

One of the nurses ran to the bed, and with a voice of
authority, she said, "Pastor, in the name of Him you have
been telling me about, I command you to stop this hyper-
ventilation."

I was so surprised to hear her use these words that I
must have just stared at her. She said it again with even
more authority: "Pastor, in the name of Him you've been
telling me about, I command you to stop this hyper-ven-
tilating."

I stopped, and the awareness came that my work was

not done for the Lord. He had even used me here in this hospital to talk to my nurses, and now one had been able to minister to me.

The goodness of God, and the warmth of the Lord began to course through my body, and I knew I was going to be all right.

In a few days, all my symptoms were gone. Slowly, but surely, my temperature returned to normal. My heart had stabilized, and the double pneumonia was gone. My veins were normal again, and there were no signs of any blood clots.

One of the most precious sights that I saw after the Lord brought me back, was the look on Betty's face. She was so happy, she was bubbling over with *Praise the Lord!*

I know if I was the poorest man on earth financially, I would still be one of the wealthiest, because I have a woman like her for my wife. Because of her obedience, intercessory prayer for me went up across this nation. I know now that God's mind can be changed if His people seek Him out and pray hard enough and long enough.

Before I was finally released from the hospital, thirty-three days passed, thirteen of them in the intensive care unit. It was with a grateful heart that I came home and took my children in my arms. I had come very close to not seeing them again, and I was thankful to the Lord that He was giving me another chance to take care of my family.

Oh, yes, there is one more part to the story.

When Pastor Wilkerson returned from Mexico City, he had an interesting tale to tell. On their first day in Mexico, a Jewish man walked into the meeting. His name was Arthur Sedinger, and he had become completed in Christ twenty years ago in the Catholic church. Now he asked for the infilling of the Holy Spirit, which the Lord promptly gave him.

The conference now had a Spirit-filled Jew who spoke to

the people about the love and goodness of Jesus. He stood in front of that congregation and told them how his Messiah had come into his life. And he didn't have to speak through an interpreter as I would have had to do. He stood in front of the people and spoke to them in flawless Spanish.

The Lord had let me know just how indispensable I really was —

The doctor had told me that it would probably take me six months of convalescence before I could resume my regular routine. I have to confess it was a pleasure renewing my ties with my family.

At first the children didn't seem to know how to take having a daddy around again. They were looking forward to summer vacation and I had promised that I would take them down to our trailer parked in Ensenada, Mexico.

I was also looking forward to this time of complete relaxation, with no phones to ring and no clocks for any of us to punch.

The moment school was out in June, the Esses family was headed down Mexico way. Our twenty-seven-foot-long trailer is parked right on the beach in Ensenada. We have had it for years, but really very little opportunity to enjoy it.

I love to go to Ensenada, because there I can go totally native. All I wear is a pair of shorts, and I don't shave at all. Betty says that none of my students would even recognize me.

The only thing we were remotely concerned about as we drove into that little Mexican town was my health. We were praying that I wouldn't have any need for medical care. We knew they wouldn't have modern medical facilities, so we were trusting the Lord to keep me well.

Little did we know that it was another member of the family for whom we should have been praying.

One evening after supper we were all in the living room

of the trailer. Betty was reading Jack London's *The Call of the Wild* out loud to us. John and Laurie were sitting on the edge of their seats, waiting to hear what would happen to Buck next.

All of a sudden, there was a loud slam, and we looked up in time to see Kathy sail out of the front door. She had leaned against the door, and it had opened because of her weight.

She landed head first, right onto a cement patio. When her head hit the cement, it sounded like a ripe watermelon being smashed open.

A tidal wave of shock hit us all. I felt like every one of us was moving in slow motion, even me.

Laurie took one look out the door at her sister lying still in a pool of blood, and a bloodcurdling scream came from her lips. "She's dead! She's dead!" she screamed, and ran for the bedroom. John was right behind her, scared to death.

As I lifted Kathy's unconscious body into the trailer, I could hear the voice of God in my ear. "Pray for her, Mike. You pray for other people to be healed. Now pray for your own child." Until this happened, I hadn't realized that I didn't pray for my own. I had enough faith for others; now I had to have enough faith for my own. One more lesson to learn.

Betty was stoic. As she wrapped Kathy in a blanket, there was not a trace of emotion on her face. She very quietly called John and Laurie, told them to get in the car, got in herself, and held out her arms for me to hand Kathy to her.

I drove like a maniac down the miserable road to the nearest hospital. In no more than ten minutes from the time Kathy fell out the door, she was on the table in the emergency room.

Fortunately, the doctor was able to speak English, so we

were able to understand him as he examined our child. He said there was no doubt that a concussion was present, as no one could hit that hard without having one.

Kathy was beginning to regain consciousness. She started to whimper and cry and move her head back and forth. Betty came and cradled her head against her breast as the doctor examined the wound.

His next words were quite a surprise to us. He said, "She'll have to be sewed up, of course, and she should be in the hospital for at least forty-eight hours for observation, but none of these things can be done here." He continued, "This is a social security hospital, and we are not allowed to treat other patients."

Through clenched teeth Betty said, "What are we supposed to do, let her bleed to death?" The doctor replied, "No, you'll have to take her to the civil hospital across town." He then proceeded to tell us how to get there.

During the ride to the civil hospital, I kept looking at Betty. I could see that it was just a matter of time before she fell completely to pieces. She was like a volcano that was going to erupt any moment. I was praying that the Lord would sustain her until the crisis was over.

The attendants took one look at us as we walked in the door of the civil hospital, and they directed us to the emergency room. Both Betty and I were covered with blood, and Kathy looked like a disaster area.

The nurses laid Kathy on the examining table while they ran to get a doctor. He came in and bent over my daughter to examine her. In a few minutes he stood up, looked at Betty and me, shrugged his shoulders, and walked out of the room. He was shaking his head, saying something that sounded like "loco gringos."

The nurses stepped back from the table, and just looked at us. It was as if they were saying, "It's your move now."

Betty and I both reached for Kathy at the same time, and

became aware of what was puzzling the doctor and nurses. When I had picked this child up off that cement, the back of her head had a bump on it the size of an orange. The gash in the middle of that lump was at least two inches long, and very deep.

Now, when we looked at her head, there was no bump, no break in the skin, and there certainly was no place where all this blood could have come from.

God had performed His surgery, and He had done it between hospitals. There was a medical confirmation of His miracle, because the first doctor had seen the wound.

We were floating on air when we returned to our car. John and Laurie were expecting us to leave Kathy in the hospital. When they saw she was with us, they squealed with delight, and oh, what a boost for their faith in the Lord when they learned she had been healed.

When we returned to the trailer, we put all the children to bed. They were so excited, they couldn't go to sleep for quite a while, but finally they dropped off. Betty had put Kathy in the front room with us, so we could look after her.

As we sat and watched our sleeping child, we talked about what a blessing she had been to our family.

Many people would look at Kathy's life and say, "What a waste," but Betty and I praise God for the privilege of having her. As her parents, we have had to grow up to the responsibility of taking care of her. And her brother and sister, John and Laurie, have learned compassion.

I have given Kathy's condition much thought, and I've come to many conclusions. First, I see in Kathy what I wish for in my other children, happiness and contentment. She is truly a happy child. She has a limited vocabulary, but "Praise the Lord," and "Jesus" are some of her words, which means she knows the most important sounds any of us can make.

This past year at Thanksgiving, the Lord put many

people across this country on a three-day fast for Kathy. Everywhere I would go to preach, the Lord would quicken this fast to the hearts of His people.

Since the end of this fast, there has been a steady improvement in our child. For years I have maintained that Kathy will some day stand with me in front of a congregation and tell of her total healing. This conviction has become stronger and stronger as time goes by.

I wish you could all know our little girl, for she is truly a joy. One of her teachers asked Betty how in the world we punished Kathy when she was naughty. Betty told her we just gave her a bop on the behind.

The teacher said, "But, Mrs. Esses, the other day I spanked her hand for touching something she had been told not to touch." Betty said, "That's good." The teacher interrupted Betty with, "But you don't understand. Kathy came back from crying, took my hand, kissed it, and said, 'Thank you.' Now how do you punish a child like that?"

The true beauty of a child like Kathy is that there is only one thing you can ever do for her, only one thing she'll ever require of you, only one thing you can ever give her. You just love her—only love her, truly love her, and you've fulfilled every need she has on this earth.

18

IT IS time to leave Athens and continue on the rest of our tour. As beautiful as Greece is, some of its beauty has been dimmed for our people with Irvine's death. I know most of them will feel better when we are on our way again.

I have called a meeting with Don Pierotti and Mahlon McCourry for this morning because I have a problem about the next stop on our agenda, Beirut, Lebanon. Betty and I are not permitted to visit Lebanon, because last year we were arrested at the Beirut airport as spies.

It all started back home in Anaheim as we laid out the annual tour for the Melodyland School of the Bible. Last year we were including the city of Cairo, Egypt.

I had told Irvine it had always been the desire of my heart to see Egypt. I love the Arabic music, and I wanted to see the culture.

I remember Betty laughing at me at the time. She said, "Mike, you sound like the Jews that Moses led out of Egypt. They were always yelling about wanting to go back, too." There was more than a little truth in Betty's jest.

I was teaching several courses in the Old Testament at this time. Once our itinerary, which included Egypt, was announced, many of my students came to me with Scripture that had been given to them to give to me.

These people were from different classes, and none of them were acquainted with the others. Yet each one of these people had been given the same Scripture. It was Jeremiah 42:19, "The Lord hath said concerning you, O ye remnant of Judah; Go ye not into Egypt: know certainly that I have admonished you this day." As I read even further in the chapter, I saw that the punishment for disobeying the admonition of the Lord was death.

As each subsequent warning was given, I began to take heed. I knew this must be the Lord, because of the confirmation from many different sources. Finally, Betty and I talked it over and made our decision.

At two o'clock in the morning, we were on the phone to the airlines finding out the cost and setting up the reservations detouring us around Egypt.

I was told it would cost $386 for Betty and me to depart from the tour and fly from Rome to Lebanon, bypassing Egypt. The rest of the tour would go from Rome to Egypt and then meet us in Lebanon.

I was concerned about the money, but Betty said if the Lord tells you not to go and you choose to be obedient, then He will supply the means for you to obey Him.

Consequently, when we were in Rome, I should have been obedient and purchased my tickets for Lebanon. But I did not.

Two things still stood in my way. I hated to spend the money, and I had a strong desire to see Egypt. When I told Betty of my decision to go on to Cairo, she was furious with me, but I wouldn't listen to her, My mind was made up.

That afternoon found us on the plane heading for Cairo. It wasn't long after the wheels left the ground that the panic set in. "Oh, Mike, you've done it again. Here you are, 20,000 feet up in the air, heading for forbidden territory in complete disobedience to your Lord."

There was no way out. When the plane sat down, I knew

I would be a doomed man. Betty could see that I was being enveloped with fear, and she tried to be helpful. "We won't go through immigration," she suggested, "we'll just stay in the airport until we can get a plane out of there."

I knew that wouldn't work, because I would have still gone into Egypt as I had been warned not to do. I started to pray and ask the Lord to forgive my disobedience. I asked for a miracle so I would be able to obey Him.

At that moment, He parted the waters for me.

There was a click as the intercom was turned on, and the pilot's voice came through with an announcement.

"Due to a small malfunction, we are going to be setting down in Athens, Greece, for about one-half hour. There is nothing to be concerned about; this will be just a short delay. Thank you."

Betty and I looked at each other in amazement. The Lord was giving us a second chance to obey Him. I was so excited I didn't even heed the "Fasten your seat belts" sign. I just rushed back to Irvine and told him Betty and I were going to get off. We'd see him in Beirut.

When the plane landed, we were off it as fast as possible. We weren't able to get our luggage. It was still going to Egypt. Well, better the luggage than me.

The plane was on the ground only the one-half hour the pilot said it would be; then they were off again, this time minus two grateful passengers.

As we stood watching the plane climb back into the sky, I knew what a close call this had been. It was again brought home to me about how patient the Lord is with us. I knew He must be wondering how many more times He was going to have to pick *me* up.

When I glanced over at Betty, she was looking at me with this perplexed expression on her face. "What's wrong?" I asked. She just shook her head and said, "Mike, whatever else being married to you is, it sure isn't dull." Then with a sigh, she sat down on her cosmetic case, folded her arms, and said, "What now?"

I realized for the first time that we were by ourselves, in a strange country. There were no reservations made, and we didn't know where we were going to sleep that night.

I obtained tickets for a flight to Lebanon the next afternoon; then we solicited help to find a hotel room from the first cab driver we found who could speak English.

We ended up staying in a hotel by the airport that just happened to be directly in the glide path for all planes taking off from Athens. You haven't lived until you've had a 747 fly through your bedroom.

Each time one of those planes would fly over, our bed would creep across the room on the wings of the vibrations. Betty and I finally got the giggles, and as the room would begin to fill with the roar of the planes we would be sitting up, riding our bed from wall to wall, laughing like a couple of fools.

The next day found us bleary-eyed, but we were on our flight to Lebanon. When we arrived in Beirut it was late afternoon. I was anxious to get through immigration and get to our hotel where I was planning to order the best Arabic meal on the menu. Betty and I both adore Arabic food, and we were really looking forward to indulging ourselves.

Unfortunately, I had not reckoned with the tension that the Arab-Israeli conflict had engendered. I quite innocently lit the fuse when, as Betty delicately puts it, I opened my big mouth.

We were going through the line at immigration, and naturally I had to use my knowledge of Arabic in this country. I greeted the soldiers who were inspecting our passports in my fluent Arabic.

Because Arabic was my home language as a child, I don't

speak it like an American would. My Syrian dialect is as distinctive to a fellow Arab, as a Southern drawl is to an American. The minute I opened my mouth, they even knew what town in Syria my family came from.

Within seconds, several of the soldiers were clustered together perusing my passport. There were various factors that made me look mighty suspicious. As I listened to them talk back and forth, I knew all these peculiarities were being stacked against me.

First, my face looks like the map of Israel; there is no doubting my Hebrew heritage. Second, I have an American passport, but I speak Arabic like a native. Third, because I had led a tour the year before, I had an Israeli stamp on my passport.

As each of these points were brought up and discussed by the soldiers, I began to have a feeling of foreboding. It wasn't long before this feeling was justified.

The soldier in charge asked us to leave the line and accompany him. We were escorted to a small room and left alone. There were no windows, just the four walls, a desk, and two chairs.

I hated to look into Betty's eyes, because I knew she was as afraid as I, and at the moment there wasn't much I could do about it. I just put my arm around her, and told her to start praying. She said, "I haven't stopped since you said hello to the first soldier."

I sat Betty down in a chair, and walked nonchalantly around the room. As I approached the door, my heart began to pound. I casually turned my back to the door, and with my hand behind my back, I tried the knob. It wouldn't turn.

I didn't tell Betty for a moment. She asked me, "Mike, is the door locked?" I nodded yes, and went over and sat beside her.

We both just sat there for quite a while, each one immersed in his own thoughts, and both of us wondering what the other was thinking.

Later, when we could talk about it, we told each other about our thoughts. It's amazing how the masculine and feminine mind differ.

I was thinking, "There is no one who even knows we're here. No one knows what plane we took. No one knows when we left or when we arrived. There will be no one to even inquire for a couple of days until the rest of the group arrives."

Now I started making plans for how I could prove who I was, and what I was doing in Beirut. I thought, "First I'll ask to speak to the American Embassy. Then I'll have the Embassy contact the travel agency to vouch for me." I began to feel better as I thought of solid moves I could make when the soldiers came back to the room.

Meanwhile, Betty said she was thinking along these lines. "I wonder if they'll offer me a last cigarette? If they do, I'll take it even though I don't smoke. Gee, I hope the blindfold matches my dress. I don't want to look tacky." This shows the basic personality of the nut I'm married to. She claimed she refused to take what was happening seriously, even to herself.

Betty explained, "Mike, the Lord had performed a miracle to get you here. I knew He wasn't going to abandon us now. So I just thought silly shallow thoughts while I praised Him for how He was going to get us out of this jackpot."

Two hours went by before the doors opened and a soldier who was identified as a captain began to question me.

Before he had too much to say, I told him that I would like to call the American Embassy so they could vouch for who I was. He said, that wouldn't be necessary, and continued to question me.

Was I an American spy? Was I an Israeli spy? Was I a Syrian spy? Did I work for the American government? Who sent me to Beirut? What was my mission?

This continued for quite a while, and it was obvious that the captain didn't believe a word I said.

Finally he left the room, only to return shortly with a man he said was Colonel of Intelligence. After we talked for a few minutes, the colonel pointed to the plastic name tag I was wearing with Reverend Michael Esses written on it.

He asked me, "Are you a priest of our faith?" I replied, "I'm a minister of the Gospel." He asked me again, "Are you a priest of our faith?" This time I answered, "I'm a Christian." Again he asked, "Are you a priest of our faith?" Then I realized he was trying to lead me into the proper answer, so I replied, "Yes, I am a priest of your faith."

Because of my giving this answer, the colonel ordered us to be released immediately. We were handed two exit permits that we were warned not to lose, because without them we couldn't leave the country.

Betty and I gave a mutual sigh of relief as we walked out into the late afternoon sun. We got a taxi to the hotel, and I placed a call to our agency representative, Mr. Bibi, telling him what had happened. He was full of apologies and promises to look into the matter.

That evening, sitting out on the terrace of the hotel, we had a beautiful Arabic meal. In a very general tone of conversation we talked with the waiters about life in their country. The only phrase that still sticks in my mind from that night is that they feel they have two enemies in this world, Satan and the Jews.

I know the events of this day were allowed by God to show me how close a call I had through my disobedience.

Lebanon is a country that is 60 percent Christian and 40 percent Moslem, even though its culture is Arabic. They are not at war with Israel. Can you imagine if I had this kind of reception in Beirut, what would have happened in Cairo, which is in a strictly Moslem country, anti-Jewish, anti-Christian, and anti-American? They also have a war-like attitude toward Israel.

When the rest of our group joined us in Beirut, they told us of the Mideast tension they experienced. As their airplane approached Egypt, a military plane joined it, flying just above until they started their descent to Cairo.

They looked up in the streets and saw guns on the tops of the buildings. Artifacts had been removed from museums, and sandbags were placed around large displays to protect them from bombings.

Egypt was a country on total alert, and they probably wouldn't have put up with this Jewish boy for one moment.

Before we left Lebanon, the Lord also showed me that I could trust Him in one more way.

Mr. Bibi, our agent, practically hand-delivered Betty and me through immigration when we left Beirut. He was there to make sure nothing went wrong. As we said good-bye to him, he thrust a check for $180 into my hand to cover the price of the tickets from Athens to Beirut. He said his agency wanted to make up in some way for the experience we had been through.

Remember Betty saying the Lord would take care of the cost if I was willing to obey Him? I'll give her credit — she didn't say, "I told you so." All she did, as I motioned her through the gate, was grin from ear to ear and give me a big wink.

I had a problem concerning the next stop on our tour, inasmuch as the State Department had requested that Betty and I not return to Lebanon. I had been counting on Irvine to see our group through while we flew direct to Tel Aviv from Athens.

I was happy that Don Pierotti was along because he had gone with us the previous year. Don could be depended upon. He and Mahlon assumed responsibility for the group and freed Betty, the children, and me to go to Tel Aviv without concern.

Mahlon even remarked that the Lord had impressed him that he was going on this trip to minister to the ministers. How right he was.

19

IT IS morning. Betty, the children, and I are saying our brief good-byes to our group. We'll be with them in a couple of days when they join us in Israel, but I can't help feeling like a mother hen. However, even though I feel I should be with the group in Lebanon, I'm glad it's been taken out of my hands. For I need a couple of days to get my balance.

The part of the trip where I will be needed most is ahead of us. Most of our days will be spent in Israel, with much teaching being done. I will have to fill a double yoke with Irvine gone, and the responsibility is heavy upon me.

As our plane approaches Tel Aviv through crystal blue skies, I remember my first visit here three years ago. We had left our children at home with our dear friends Jean and Charles Marshall. Jean had helped with Kathy for years, so we knew our children were being beautifully cared for.

It was only a few months since Donnie's death, and my emotions were still very raw.

I had looked to the day when I would put my feet on the land of my ancestors since I was a child. That yearly prayer that ends the Passover with "And next year in Jerusalem," had placed in me the heritage of longing for this city.

I remember now that a new element was there that I

did not know would manifest itself until the wheels of the plane hit the ground in Israel.

I had always expected that if I ever set foot in Israel it would be as a Jew. A Jew that the blood of his forefathers would cry out to from this promised land.

I felt I would be a Jew whose land had been returned to him after 2,000 years. I know the thrill that I had felt in 1948 when Israel became a sovereign state once again. I was proud, proud of God and proud to be of a people who had persevered.

Yet when the plane landed in Tel Aviv, it was not a Jew who emerged and kissed the ground of his people. It was not a Jew whose eyes filled with tears and whose heart ached with gratitude.

It was a completed Jew who landed in Israel. One who knew his Messiah, and revered this land for no other reason than that Christ had lived here. That was the new element. That was the overwhelming feeling.

It was not my ancestors who were important to me, it was Christ. I looked around this small country and down every dusty road, and I saw that small band of men trudging down every path. That God Himself had trod this land, ministering and teaching with His small group of disciples, was the miracle of miracles to me.

As I went about this land of Canaan, Christ walked with me every inch of the way. I looked around me and knew I was walking where He had been born, had been a young boy, a man, finally crucified, but most important of all, resurrected.

That was what was important, His resurrection. Because of it, He walked with me then and is with me now.

Standing on the Mount of Olives, looking down at the Golden Gate, my thoughts went back to the teachings of my father and the rabbis. I knew what they told me was true, that the day would come when the Messiah would come through that gate in triumph—King of kings and Lord of lords.

What I truly love Him for, though, is not His expected triumphant return, but that He loved me enough to come as a helpless babe, so that I may live with Him forever.

I wish my fellow Hebrews could know the amount of love it took for God to sacrifice His only begotten Son for them. His faithfulness to a people who were so unfaithful to Him is a monument to forgiveness and love.

It seemed no matter where I wandered in this land the travail of Christ followed me. I was a completely broken man the entire time I was in Israel.

The depth of His suffering was brought home in a vivid way the day that we went to the Garden of Gethsemane. As I knelt in prayer, the thought of the anguish Jesus had to endure for me overcame me, and I began to weep.

Jesus the man knew the suffering He would have to endure. The salvager of Israel would have to be mocked, spat upon, and bear the cross. It is hard for a mortal such as I to even imagine a love that could submit itself to such agony.

Throughout that trip, every place I went, the agony of Christ was present until we arrived at the Sea of Galilee. Betty and I slipped away from the rest of the group and walked down to the water's edge by ourselves.

We were both trying hard to control our feelings. So far, the trip had been hard, because every place we went we were feeling for God for the suffering of His Son, as we had suffered the loss of ours.

Now here at the Sea of Galilee, where Jesus quieted the storm for His disciples, He stilled the storm for Betty and me.

As we stood there looking over that calm sea, a wind blew up, and in seconds the waves were pounding against the rocks at our feet.

Because the turmoil happened so fast, we were taken aback in alarm, but just as fast, the wind ceased, and the sea was like glass again. With this calm, came a prevailing feeling of peace, love, and gentleness all around us.

It was as if Jesus had taken us in His arms and held us close while He poured the oil of acceptance and peace over our hearts. I felt He was saying, "I accepted the loss of my Son; now I want you to accept the loss of yours."

By this time Betty and I were crying out the grief that had come into us again, because of the grief we felt here in Jerusalem. We realized we were missing the final chapter of the book. God's Son arose, and so did ours.

The rebellion in me is finally broken, but not with beatings. This stiff neck has finally bowed before love. Love is the answer. The Lord has supplied me with love all my life.

Many times I thrust it aside, but Jesus kept on loving me no matter how obnoxious I became.

The Lord loved me enough not to give up on me. He loved me enough to deal with me over and over—until I was able to come into *HIS Promised Land.*

FOR A
FREE SAMPLE COPY
OF
LOGOS JOURNAL
WRITE
BOX 191
PLAINFIELD, N.J. 07060